UNDERSTANDING BEHAVIORAL SCIENCE

RESEARCH METHODS FOR RESEARCH CONSUMERS

P9-ARR-856

UNDERSTANDING BEHAVIORAL SCIENCE

RESEARCH METHODS FOR RESEARCH CONSUMERS

Ralph L. Rosnow
Temple University

Robert Rosenthal
Harvard University

McGraw-HILL BOOK COMPANY

New York St. Louis San Francisco Auckland Bogotá
Hamburg Johannesburg London Madrid Mexico Montreal New Delhi
Panama Paris São Paulo Singapore Sydney Tokyo Toronto

This book was set in Times Roman by Emanon Typesetting Inc.
The editor was David V. Serbun;
the production supervisor was Diane Renda.
The cover was designed by Anne Canevari Green.
Project supervision was done by The Book Studio Inc.
R. R. Donnelley & Sons Company was printer and binder.

300.72

R822

UNDERSTANDING BEHAVIORAL SCIENCE

Research Methods for Research Consumers

2 3 4 5 6 7 8 9 0 DOCDOC 8 9 8 7 6 5 4

ISBN 0-07-053809-3

Library of Congress Cataloging in Publication Data

Rosnow, Ralph L.
   Understanding behavioral science.

   Bibliography: p.
   Includes index.
   1. Psychology—Research—Methodology.   2. Social
sciences—Research—Methodology.   I. Rosenthal, Robert,
date   . II. Title.
BF76.5.R65   1984   300'.72   83-13600
ISBN 0-07-053809-3

To Mimi and Mary Lu

CONTENTS

PREFACE

Our purpose in this book is to convey a sense of the logic and meaning of the technical concepts associated with the application of the scientific method in the study of human relations. We have designed this book for use in introductory courses in psychology, education, communication, social psychology, business, and other behavioral and social sciences in which a basic understanding of the research process is essential in order to assess the usefulness (and limitations) of empirical investigations.

We have used this material in our own courses to introduce new psychology majors to the application of research methods in the social sciences. We have also used portions of the book as collateral reading material in a nonquantitative introduction for M.A. students in a program of study that required skill in the understanding (rather than in the actual practice) of behavioral research. We assume no prior knowledge of any quantitative procedures beyond what is now taught in junior high school. The reader or instructor who is interested in a more detailed and advanced treatment of research methods might refer to our other textbook, *Essentials of Behavioral Research: Methods and Data Analysis*.

There is also a wider audience to whom this book is addressed—those readers beyond the formal classroom who learn about research in newspapers and magazines. All of us, students or not, are affected in our daily lives by a knowledge (or lack of knowledge) of basic principles of research methods. It can cost us dearly not to understand these basic principles, for example, when watching, hearing, or reading advertisements or news stories based on research claims. It is important to cultivate at least a rudimentary understanding of the scientific method in order not to fall victim to false claims based on "bad science."

It is also, of course, important for the decision maker to be aware of where in the published literature there is research knowledge that can be of considerable use in guiding one's choices. In recent years, a number of computerized literature searches have been developed which incorporate different data bases of bibliographic compilations. For example, there is MED-LARS, which was developed by the Department of Health, Education, and Welfare in 1966 and which indexes medically related publications from several thousand journals. PASAR, developed by the American Psychological Association, indexes books and periodical journals in the social and behavioral sciences. ISI OATS, run by the Institute for Scientific Information in Philadelphia, is a retrieval service that tracks down journal articles and supplies reprints for a fee. A useful discussion of these and other literature searches and retrieval approaches can be found in William McGuire's chapters 3 and 4 in his book with Benjamin Lipstein, *Evaluating Advertising* (Advertising Research Foundation, 1978). Another good place to begin a literature search is by looking in handbooks and annual reviews and then going to the original articles for further relevant citations.

We are indebted to many colleagues who read and criticized drafts of this manuscript; among them are Frank Calabrese, Charles Halcomb, Allan Kimmel, Gordon Russell, Frank Savage, and several anonymous reviewers of the publisher. We also thank Mimi Rosnow for helpful editorial suggestions and Mary Lu Rosenthal for preparing the index of this and our other methods books. We are grateful to the National Science Foundation for support of much of the research which eventually led to our recognition of the need for this type of book, and to Temple University for support shown the first author in the form of the Bolton Professorship. John Wiley & Sons Publishers gave us permission to incorporate sections from our earlier primer of methods, and the American Psychological Association and the Rand Corporation permitted us to reprint or adapt various materials. The first author would also like to thank his teaching assistants in Psych 274, Temple University, who used portions of this book in their tutorial sections: Penny Cooke, Sue Kraus, Janice Lipsky, Mike Matthews, Nan Nelson, and Sandra Tunis.

Ralph L. Rosnow
Robert Rosenthal

UNDERSTANDING BEHAVIORAL SCIENCE

RESEARCH METHODS FOR RESEARCH CONSUMERS

NATURE OF
BEHAVIORAL RESEARCH

CHAPTER 1

BEHAVIORAL SCIENCE AND THE SCIENTIFIC METHOD

"Ask a scientist what he conceives the scientific method to be, and he will adopt an expression that is at once solemn and shifty-eyed: solemn, because he feels he ought to declare an opinion; shifty-eyed, because he is wondering how to conceal the fact that he has no opinion to declare." So wrote one eminent scientist recently (Medawar, 1969, p. 11). While that statement may apply to many scientists, it is nevertheless true that most people have at least a vague idea of what scientists do: They think, theorize, observe and do experiments, pore over data, and write reports. In this chapter and throughout this book, we attempt to state more clearly and explicitly exactly how scientists in the *behavioral sciences* go about their work. This chapter explores how behavioral scientists, using the "scientific method," try by reflection and observation to comprehend the nature of human relations.

WHAT IS BEHAVIORAL SCIENCE?

In using the term "behavioral science," we are actually referring to many fields of inquiry (or disciplines) that have traditionally been grouped together under a single heading. The behavior of early primitive human beings, humans beings as political animals, economic animals, social animals, talking animals, human beings as logicians—these are the concern of psychologists, marketing and educational researchers, sociologists, anthropologists, political scientists, communication researchers, economists, psycholinguists, behavioral biologists, and even some statisticians.

While for most purposes it probably makes little difference whether we can distinguish among these various disciplines, there are differences nonetheless. Table 1.1 illustrates one such difference—the level of emphasis or focus that historically has been the province of a particular discipline. For example, social psychology and personality psychology have traditionally concentrated on the *micro* (or more diminutive) aspects of individual and interpersonal behavior, while sociology and anthropology have traditionally looked at social and cultural variables that are *macro* (or larger) aspects of human relations. Sociologists also tend to be more interested in survey sampling and studying behavior in its natural setting than do most psychologists, who in turn tend to be more interested in performing controlled experiments in the lab than do most sociologists.

In spite of traditional boundaries, such as those shown in this table, behavioral scientists often find it useful to borrow from one another's methods and theories. Thus the boundary lines are by no means rigid. For example, to learn how social behavior is governed by cultural circumstances, psychologists have had to probe into social norms and values (historically the province of sociologists and anthropologists). Sociologists and anthropologists have also had to borrow from psychologists, in order to understand how complex interactions of societal and cultural

TABLE 1.1
LEVELS OF ANALYSIS AND THE RESPECTIVE SUBSTANTIVE AREAS THAT HAVE HISTORICALLY BEEN THE PROVINCE OF PARTICULAR DISCIPLINES

Degree of micro/macro	Unit of study	Discipline (example)
Most macro	Cultural system	Anthropology
More macro	Group or social system	Sociology
More micro	Interactions among individuals	Social psychology
Most micro	Individual personality	Personality psychology

events are influenced by individual perceptions and by interpersonal dynamics.

The point is that in order to develop a complete picture of human behavior, researchers must often develop an *interdisciplinary* understanding of their subject. Sometimes researchers will create a whole new discipline when they find a very similar combination of interdisciplinary theories, methods, concepts, and data to be useful. Examples of these hybrid disciplines in behavioral science are behavioral medicine, mathematical psychology, biosociology, sociolinguistics, psychochemistry, ethnopsychology, and psychological anthropology. Each of these boundary-melting disciplines is of relatively recent origin. These researchers hope that their hybrid fields will show the same vigor and potential for breakthrough found in the combination of formerly differentiated disciplines in other sciences.

One prime example is that of "psychological economics" (Katona, 1975, 1979). The traditional science of economics most commonly proceeds on the premise that people behave generally in the same way according to universal economic principles. For instance, the principle that "consumer expenditures are a function of income" has usually been taken to mean that all human beings will automatically spend the same proportion of their incomes without regard for individual motives or attitudes. The interdisciplinary field of psychological economics proceeds on a quite different premise; in this field it is argued that human behavior is not at all like that of a machine running with clockwork precision. Instead it is theorized that there are individual differences and human idiosyncrasies to be considered. As a result, this new field cuts across the time-honored boundaries of economics and psychology, in order to consider economic processes as a function of both individual psychology *and* economic principles.

One final point: Behavioral science (as we use the term in this book) is not simply synonymous with the view known as *methodological behaviorism*. This refers to the idea that looking for causes of behavior inside the organisms that scientists study is likely to be difficult, and for this reason behaviorists encourage researchers only to describe behavior in fully observable terms (Skinner, 1953). Only the observable relations between stimuli and responses are permissible as scientific data and there is no need to speculate about what occurs beyond these visible relations, methodological behaviorists argue. We reject this view of science as overly narrow and suggest instead that in most cases one cannot fully appreciate human relations without also going beyond what can be immediately observed.

EMPIRICISM IN SYSTEMATIC INQUIRY

Of course, not everyone who professes an interest in behavior is necessarily a behavioral scientist. Painters, novelists, philosophers, and theologians are also concerned with behavior. While they may have much of consequence to suggest to the behavioral scientist, they themselves are not behavioral scientists (nor, ordinarily, would they wish to be considered as such). It is not easy to say just how the behavioral scientist's interest in behavior differs from anyone else's, but it is possible to differentiate the *work* of the professional student of behavior from others who share such interests.

The work of the behavioral scientist is often said to be characterized by the *systematic nature* of his or her approach to questions having to do with the logic of human experience. The term "systematic" seems to imply *a particular system,* but all it really means is that the scientific method is composed of many *orderly* scientific practices, not just one system. Those who use these practices have evolved a set of formal and informal rules by which to assess their adequacy. When a substantial segment of the behavioral science community feels that some practices "work" or "pay off" or "produce," they come to be regarded as *good scientific practices.* The "scientific method" is a collective term referring to all of these systems of good scientific practices.

Nevertheless, there is one characteristic, more than any other, that identifies the work of the professional student of behavior. It is that these good scientific practices are *empirically* oriented. This means that they rely on the specific use of objective experience as opposed to relying on armchair theorizing or as opposed to holding some belief to be true simply because it has been authorized by an individual or an institution in a position of relative power. Empiricism, in fact, is a fundamental characteristic of every science, harking back to the seventeenth century, history's watershed between the ancient and modern worlds (Leary, 1980). The expression "history's watershed" indicates that almost everything distinguishing the world in which we live from the world of ancient times is attributable to science, which achieved its first spectacular triumphs in the hands of empirical researchers such as Kepler, Galileo, and Newton during that period.

Empiricism first entered the field of behavioral science in the nineteenth century, when researchers such as the English scientist and writer Francis Galton demonstrated the possibility of bringing within the empirical domain of science matters until then thought to lie completely outside its competence (Medawar, 1969). In one famous study, Galton perceived a way of establishing "scientific" grounds for testing the belief that prayers are answered. In England, the health and longevity of the royal family was something prayed for weekly on a national scale, and Galton developed the testable proposition (or *hypothesis*) that if prayers are answered, then members of the royal families must live longer as a result of prayers on their behalf. To test this hypothesis, he computed the mean age attained by various groups of adult males (excluding deaths by accident or violence) and compared these figures with the mean age attained by adult members of royal houses. Finding that the average longevity of members of royal houses was 64 years, while, for example, clergymen lived to be 69, laywers to be 68, and physicians to be 67, he concluded that, within the scientific arena in which he had examined this question, a belief in the efficacy of prayer was not justified. This is not to say that prayers cannot strengthen resolution and bring serenity. Nevertheless, the weight of evidence using the scientific method showed that in the area of longevity royalty fared worse than people of humbler birth.

REGULATIVE VERSUS EMPIRICAL PRINCIPLES

Galton did not profess to throw light on the extent to which human beings could commune with God, but sought only to address the question whether there were any empirical grounds for the formidable authority of prayer. Some principles, he realized, were simply beyond the scope of empirical observation. It is true that in every science there are assumptions that go beyond what can be scientifically corroborated. These nonempirical assumptions (sometimes called *regulative principles* by philosophers—Apel, 1981, 1982) provide scientists with vantage points from which to concretize or objectify what otherwise might be dismissed as a succession of accidental events without substance or purpose. (*Empirical principles,* on the other hand, are those that can be empirically tested and corroborated by the use of scientific methods.)

Take, for instance, the interdisciplinary field of social psychology. In social psychology, there are assumptions made that, while not empirical principles, give meaning to the relationships between and within empirical principles explaining the logic of social behavior. One important regulative principle is that humans are sociocentric (or "social animals"), by which it is meant that society is "wired into" human nature. There is ample indirect or circumstantial evidence for this regulative principle in the artifacts and other such remains of prehistoric peoples and their cultures to suggest that there never was a period on earth when human beings did not interact in groups and societies. It is also true, of course, that habitual destruction of members of the human species has been a fact of life throughout history. Humans may be social animals, but social behavior also seems to be full of egocentrism, rationalism, and irrationalism among other apparent contradictions. The point is that regulative principles such as these imply their own standards that in part go beyond the visible relations between human beings.

EMPIRICAL PRINCIPLES: "PROBABILISTIC ASSERTIONS"

The empirical principles of behavioral and social science, on the other hand, are *probabilistic assertions* that have been inferred on the basis of observable facts. That is to say, they are based on assumed probabilities; which means that the scientist assumes, based on empirical evidence, that a particular generalization dealing with relatively uncertain events is likely to be correct over the long run. The term "probability" refers to the mathematical chance of an event occurring. At a race track we see horses that are "20 to 1 shots." This presumably means that in the eyes of the odds setters that particular long shot will win about once in every 21 races, given the conditions under which the horse is currently running. Why should a horse ever beat other horses that are faster than it is? Because of the relative uncertainty in the actions that determine the outcome of a horse race. The lead horse might stumble; the jockey on the second horse might fall off; and so forth. Unlikely? Yes—but, that is why the track management is willing to pay 20 to 1 odds (Lana & Rosnow, 1972).

This example gives us two ideas about probabilistic assertions: (*a*) they deal with uncertainty; (*b*) they are long-term but not permanent generalizations. There are few permanent or "invariant generalizations" in behavioral science, in the sense that there are laws in physics such as Newton's laws of motion or Einstein's $E = mc^2$. The reason for this is that most of the observable facts of behavioral science can be influenced by human intention, by chance events, and by historical circumstances that may be constantly changing. This introduces variability and relative uncertainty into the empirical principles of behavior, hence the need for probabilistic assertions. An example would be the empirical principle that "frustration leads to aggression" or that "similarity leads to attraction." The implication of such generalizations is that there is ample empirical evidence for belief that, under specifiable conditions, they are *probably correct over a long term.*

Typically, as in the examples above, the assumed probability of an empirical generalization is not explicitly given, but is implicit. When drawing specific conclusions on the basis of empirical data, however, the odds that a particular conclusion is likely to be true may be explicitly given in the way that the odds setter said that a horse was a "20 to 1 shot" or in the way that weather reports include a statement like: "There is a 70 percent probability of rain tomorrow." Does this mean that it is going to rain for 70 percent of the day? No, it means that, when examined over the long run, 70 percent of all days that follow weather characteristics like today have been rainy. In the same way, an opinion pollster who makes specific inferences from survey samples will also state the long-term probability that opinions in the population at large are similar to those in the sample of responses. The researcher might make a statement like: "In 95 cases out of 100 the results based on the entire sample differ by no more than 2 percentage points in either direction from what would have been obtained by interviewing everyone in the population."

WHAT CONSTITUTES A "GOOD" HYPOTHESIS?

Empirical principles typically originate as *working hypotheses* to guide and organize the scientist's research. That is, they are untested ideas used by researchers to give shape and direction to their inquiry. To illustrate, Bibb Latané and John Darley (1970) developed their diffusion-of-responsibility hypothesis as a working idea to guide and organize their empirical investigation of some perplexing behavior they had heard reported. A young woman named Kitty Genovese had been viciously murdered, and not a single person had come to her aid in spite of the fact that her cries of terror were heard by at least three dozen of her neighbors. She died before anyone ever bothered to telephone the police, even though the murderer took over a half hour to kill her.

Puzzled by this frightening passivity on the part of the victim's neighbors, Latané and Darley set out to discover why *so many* people failed to intervene. There are several ways in which witnesses or bystanders can make each individual who is present less likely to act, Latané and Darley reasoned. They hypothesized that each bystander could be picking up cues which in turn could produce a diffusion of individual personal responsibility. They used this hypothesis to explain why no one came to Kitty Genovese's assistance, and they tested it in many laboratory and field experiments. In these experiments they were able realistically to simulate a threatening incident while at the same time to vary the number of people present. As a consequence of these investigations, they were eventually able to restate their hypothesis as an empirical principle asserting that *social respon- sibility is likely to be dissipated whenever many people are pre- sent during an emergency.*

This example also points out how scientists view facts not as isolated or separate entities or events, but as meaningfully con- nected. The scientist's working hypothesis is the starting point for approaching this sort of connectedness, by making a theoretical guess as to the significance or meaning of a given fact (Cohen, 1959). The ability to develop *good* hypotheses—by which we mean fruitful research ideas that are both testable and worthy of scientific consideration—is an acquired skill.

How can we recognize a "good hypothesis"? Besides the ob- vious requirement that it be testable, another characteristic of a good hypothesis is that it has been subjected to the scientist's intellectual ruminative and winnowing process to "cut away" what is superfluous. Known as the *principle of parsimony* or *Occam's razor* (after William of Occam, the fourteenth-century Franciscan philosopher), the ideal hypothesis is a statement of research ideas in as simple and straightforward a way as possible, so as not to overcomplicate the search for truth.

Another characteristic of a good hypothesis is that it typically has a reasonably high *antecedent probability.* "Antecedent" means prior to or going before, and to have a high antecedent probability means that the working hypothesis is believed, even before being empirically tested, to be sound and likely to prove *relevant* to the problem under investigation. Scientists rely on common sense and experience, and they try to avoid the fallacy inherent in the *drunkard's search* (Kaplan, 1964). It seems that a drunkard lost his house key, and he began searching for it under a street lamp although he had dropped the key some distance away. When asked why he didn't look where he had dropped it, he replied, "It's lighter here!" Like the drunkard's search, much effort can be lost or wasted when the researcher looks in a conve- nient place but not in the most likely one. Whether it be a key or some vital scientific evidence, it is important that the thing sought have a reasonably high antecedent probability of being in the place where the scientist is looking for it.

SERENDIPITY IN SCIENCE

Hypotheses should be parsimonious and have a reasonably high antecedent probability, to be sure, but it is also prudent to observe with a keen, attentive, inquisitive, and open mind, for sometimes valuable discoveries are made by accident. This faculty for making discoveries in the course of investigations designed for another purpose is called *serendipity,* a term derived from "Serendip," which was once the name for Sri Lanka. Horace Walpole, the eighteenth-century English novelist and essayist, claimed that the three princes of Serendip were constantly making discoveries by good luck, hence "serendipity." Luck plays a part in scientific research when the scientist hits upon a right idea based on some felicitous discovery (Cannon, 1945; Merton, 1968).

Murray Sidman (1960) has mentioned an example in behavioral science in the behind-the-scenes story of a series of experiments that came to be known as the "ulcer project." It started with experiments that were being performed by Joseph V. Brady in his laboratory at Walter Reed Army Hospital. Brady was running experiments with monkeys using long-term conditioning and electric shocks, food reinforcements, and brain stimulation. There was an unusually high mortality rate among the monkeys, which the researchers might have continued to treat simply as an unavoidable problem were it not for an accidental discovery. R. W. Porter, a pathologist, was also working at Walter Reed, and when he heard about the large number of deaths, he asked Brady for permission to do a post-mortem on the next few monkeys that became available. During the next few months, Porter would occasionally appear in Brady's office holding a piece of freshly excised monkey gut. Somewhere in the tissue there would be a clear round hole, which (Porter would explain to Brady) was a perforated ulcer.

One day, however, Porter remarked that of several hundred monkeys that he had examined before coming to Walter Reed, not one had shown any sign of a normally occurring ulcer. This remark was enough to cause Brady to change the course of his research. Could the ulcers have had something to do with the role the monkeys were obliged to play in the stress situation? Brady began doing experiments in which monkeys were subjected to electric-shock avoidance training and were paired with other monkeys who received the same shocks but without the opportunity to avoid them. When the monkeys were finally sacrificed, there were the stomach ulcers in the monkeys who had been called upon to make "executive" decisions in the stress situation, while the "subordinate" monkeys showed no unusual pathology (Brady, 1958; Brady, Porter, Conrad, & Mason, 1958). This led to extensive further research to pinpoint the precise causes of this effect, and eventually to new insights about the limitations of the findings of the ulcer project.

Serendipity has to be exploited, as Brady and others have shown. The lucky find must be noticed, explored, and interpreted for it to contribute to the body of scientific knowledge (Kaplan, 1964). Scientists, being human and fallible, may sometimes act on their preconceptions rather than on what is apparent to the naked eye. Because it is important to approach science with a clear and open mind, scientists are taught to look for *plausible rival hypotheses*. This important concept (which we shall refer to again) means that instead of becoming attached to a single working hypothesis, the scientist considers reasonable alternatives that rival the working hypothesis as an explanation for the occurrence of the specified phenomenon (Campbell & Stanley, 1966). It is important that the scientist not let a kind of "parental affection" for an idea blind him or her to the truth, or soon scientists will find themselves shaping the facts to make them fit their hypotheses (Chamberlin, 1897).

SUMMARY

We have begun to look at how behavioral scientists use the "scientific method" to study human relations. The term is a misnomer, however, since science employs many empirical methods (not just one method), which provide scientists with logical and systematic ways to conduct their research. The term "behavioral science" is also something of a misnomer, since it is a shorthand expression for many independent and interdisciplinary fields of inquiry that use the scientific method to study behavior. Regulative and empirical principles are the cornerstones of all science, but it is only empirical principles that are scientifically testable. These principles typically begin as working hypotheses, and through the use of the scientific method evolve into the types of probabilistic assertions which state the tenets of human relations.

KEY TERMS

behavioral science
empiricism
good scientific practices
high antecedent probability
hypothesis (or working hypothesis)
interdisciplinary approach
macro- versus micro-orientation
methodological behaviorism
plausible rival hypotheses
principle of parsimony (Occam's razor)
principle of the drunkard's search
probabilistic assertion
regulative versus empirical principles
serendipity
systematic research

CHAPTER 2

RESEARCH VARIABLES AND CAUSALITY

It is a convenience to be able to refer abstractly to the material or objective things that behavioral scientists observe or measure or plan to investigate as *variables*. In this chapter, we distinguish between the dependent variable and the independent variable, and the principal ways by which these variables are defined. We also discuss the problem of how researchers logically infer what is the cause, what is the effect, and how one type of variable proceeds from the other.

INDEPENDENT AND DEPENDENT VARIABLES

The *dependent variable* refers to the response or reaction to some identifiable cause or antecedent condition in which the researcher is interested. The *independent variable* refers to the cause or antecedent condition on which the dependent variable depends. Changes in the independent variable, usually symbolized as X, are thus conceived as having "led to" changes in the dependent variable, usually symbolized as Y. In the statement "jogging makes you feel better," the independent variable would be jogging status (i.e., jogging or not jogging) and the dependent variable would be feeling status (feeling better or not feeling better):

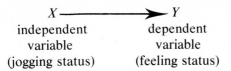

$$X \longrightarrow Y$$

independent	dependent
variable	variable
(jogging status)	(feeling status)

There are any number of different independent variables of interest to behavioral scientists. Some independent variables—biological drives and personality traits, for example—operate *internally,* "pushing" human beings in a particular direction or toward specific goals or objectives. Other independent variables—the social environment, group pressures, societal norms, etc.—operate *externally,* "pulling" people in one direction or another. Often, to be sure, it is difficult to distinguish clearly the pushes and pulls. Consider a simple example: A male dog is sexually aroused by a female in heat and as he approaches the female he becomes increasingly aroused. What are the pushes and pulls?

Although there are many other ways of classifying dependent variables, animal behaviorists often distinguish among three kinds: (*a*) the direction of behavior, (*b*) the quantity or persistence of behavior, and (*c*) the ease of behavior. For example, in a learning experiment that consisted of teaching a thirsty rat to run through a complicated maze toward a small thimbleful of water, the dependent variable could be the *direction* the rat chose on each trial, that is, whether the rat turned toward or away from water. The dependent variable could also be how long the rat *persisted* in the correct response when the water was no longer available at the end of the runway and all that greeted the rat each time was an empty thimble. A third dependent variable could be the *ease* with which the rat reacquired the correct response when the thimble of water was again made available to it.

We find dependent variables roughly analogous to these three in human research in the behavioral and social sciences. Suppose we were interested in the effects of two different types of propaganda, emotional and rational, on a person's beliefs. We could begin by observing how much the person's beliefs changed on being exposed to each type (disregarding the direction of change). This would tell us something about the relative strength of the two types of propaganda in a concrete situation. We could also measure the direction of the person's beliefs, in order to determine if there were any changes in the predicted direction as opposed to any "boomerang effects" (changes in the opposite direction of that advocated by a communicator). If we found changes, we could then track them over a period of time to see how long they persisted. We could also examine the ease with which persons were able to defend their newly acquired beliefs over time.

OPERATIONAL AND THEORETICAL DEFINITIONS

Whatever the variables, the researcher would take pains to describe them in clear and precise terms. This tells other scientists what is being studied and allows them to integrate their own or other relevant findings within the body of research, and to build on it or challenge it. It is customary to distinguish between two principal types of definitions in science, the operational and the theoretical (or conceptual)—although there are others as well (e.g., Kendler, 1981).

The *operational definition* is one that assigns meaning to a variable in terms of the operations necessary to measure it in any concrete situation. For example, the operational definition of intelligence might be stated as the "intelligence quotient" or IQ, which is a weighted composite of scores on an intelligence test such as the Stanford-Binet or the Wechsler Adult Intelligence Scales.

The notion of an operational definition was first put forward by the physicist P. W. Bridgman (1937) as a simple recipe to furnish meaningful discussion about empirical results. But Bridgman's view of operational definitions was not dogmatic. He realized that it was perfectly acceptable to speak of some variables even if there was no procedure for measuring them empirically. Physicists speak meaningfully of the "weight of an object while it is falling." However, the only instruments for measuring the object's weight empirically would require that its motion be stopped (cf. Easley, 1971).

Scientists use a *theoretical* (conceptual) *definition* to assign meaning in more abstract terms. One reason is that operational definitions can be so simple as to appear trivial. An operational definition of intelligence might be "what the intelligence test measures." Intelligence can also be conceptualized as an explicit theory of intellectual functioning. In this case, the theoretical meaning of intelligence is contained in the totality of theoretical statements (assumptions and assertions) that are proposed to explain the empirical relations involving intellectual functioning (see Kendler, 1981). A theoretical definition of intelligence would have to account for a wide range of facts and many processes such as memory, conceptual development, and so on.

PROS AND CONS OF ASSUMING LAWFUL CAUSALITY

When implying that *X is responsible for Y,* or when making prob-abilistic assertions using terms such as "cause" and "lead to," the behavioral scientist means that there is satisfactory evidence that *X* probably serves to determine *Y.* Statements of this sort are *determinative assertions,* since they imply that a particular behavior is subject to lawful determination (lawful causality). This is not an assumption with which every layperson would agree when it comes to assertions about human behavior.

Adolf Grünbaum (1952) has discussed certain objections that have been raised against the assumption of lawful causality. He has tried to show why scientists believe that they are without foundation. One argument against determinative assertions insists that human behavior is not amenable to causal description because each person is unique, or *particularistic.* Grünbaum answers that *all* particulars in the world are unique, whether they be human beings or objects like trees or events like light flashes. Every tick of the watch is unique, since no two ticks can be simultaneous with a given third event. Certainly every individual is unique by virtue of a distinctive combination of characteristics not precisely duplicated in any other individual. However, particularism (uniqueness) does not also mean unlawfulness. We can throw coins in the air and get a unique pattern. We may not be able to repeat the identical pattern, but we can state a statistical law for the particular result nonetheless.

Another argument against the assumption of lawful causality is that, even if there is a causal order, it is too complex for human behavior ever to be discovered. Human activity, it is often said, involves so complex a profusion of variables that it is impossible to unravel them. Grünbaum reminds us that similar arguments were raised against the physics of motion before the time of Galileo. Critics insisted that it was hopeless to attempt to reduce the vast complexity of terrestrial and celestial motions to a few simple laws. The development of Newtonian physics put this criticism to rest. There is no reason, many behavioral researchers believe, why the same thing may not happen in their science.

Some critics would respond that behavioral researchers are being too optimistic in their assessment of the potential of behavioral science. Nevertheless, researchers proceed on this optimistic assumption, even though they recognize that unraveling cause and effect can be an extraordinarily difficult task in behavioral science (Cohen, 1931/1959). Is feminism the cause or the effect of the greater economic opportunity open to women? Is poverty the cause or the effect of a higher birth rate? That is, does the greater number of mouths to feed in a family reduce the individual shares of the family income, or do the poor perhaps seek a hedge against their old age by having many children some of whom will be likely to care for them?

UNRAVELING CAUSE AND EFFECT

Sometimes when it is not clear from a statistical relationship that a variable is dependent or independent, we can ask ourselves what the logical sequence would be, and in this way make the determination. Suppose a researcher found a definite statistical relationship between biological gender and height, and wanted to hypothesize which was the independent variable and which the dependent variable. Logic would dictate that biological gender is more likely to determine height than that height determines biological gender, because a person's biological gender is established at birth.

Or suppose the researcher had been examining the relationship between birth order and volunteering to participate as a subject in behavioral research, and wanted to hypothesize the independent and dependent variables. In this case, it is more logical to think of birth order than of volunteering as the independent variable. It is unreasonable to think that volunteering could be a determinant of one's order of birth!

When researchers try to unravel social causes and effects in societies, however, they are dealing with more complicated relationships. This is because social variables can function equally and simultaneously as causes and effects. For example, rumors may cause riots, but riots may simultaneously cause rumors to surface—rumors can operate at the same time both as independent *and* dependent variables. In fact, rumors can also cause other rumors; a rumor can trigger needs which, in turn, cause additional rumors to proliferate in the pressure for relief. In this case, the rumor contributes to the situation, and the situation then contributes additional rumors as a result (Esposito & Rosnow, 1983; Rosnow, 1980; Rosnow & Kimmel, 1979).

Perhaps wisely, perhaps overcautiously, behavioral scientists have usually sidestepped the philosophical issues involved in unraveling social causes and effects. If pressed to say what they mean, most would probably prefer to talk about "understanding" rather than causality. However, we need only push a bit to see that understanding is a quite subjective matter. I understand a certain phenomenon and if you don't see it my way, why then you simply don't understand it. But perhaps I can show you I understand it by stating hypotheses about what will happen in the future, hypotheses based on my understanding of the independent and dependent variables. If we still do not see eye to eye, then perhaps you will also want to state some hypotheses based on your understanding. If your rival hypotheses logically imply predictions that are better borne out by the observations we make than are my hypotheses, then I am willing to concede your greater understanding of the causal factors of the phenomenon in question.

Of course, we can also try to understand behavior without thinking about what caused it. If we want to know only whether there is a relationship between two measures of racial prejudice or authoritarianism or intelligence, we would refer to them as variables but would not try to distinguish independent from dependent variables.

REQUIREMENTS FOR CAUSAL INFERENCES

David Hume, the eighteenth-century Scottish philosopher, saw that when people say that "X causes Y," they really mean that X and Y constantly go together, not that there is some necessary connection between them. In fact, he argued, people usually have no other notion than that X and Y are united in this way. Because it is possible for all objects to become causes or effects of each other, what is needed are rules of logic by which we may know when they really do serve as causes or effects, he reasoned. The rules that Hume developed were condensed by John Stuart Mill, a century later, to three essentials that provide the basic logic to begin to make causal inferences.

The first essential of any causal inference is that Y did not occur until after X. The second requirement is that X and Y are actually shown to be related. The third (and most difficult requirement) is that other explanations of the relationship between X and Y can be eliminated as plausible rival hypotheses.

Hume believed that wanting to know what leads to what suggested the need for what he called the "experimental method of reasoning," and Mill developed logical "methods" related to his three requirements that became the basis of experimental design. In Chapter 5, we turn to these methods of Mill's that have led to the belief that perhaps the only way to be sure that X leads to Y is to vary X and observe the consequences. However, sometimes it is not possible to vary X, for ethical or technical and practical reasons, in which case researchers may have to accept the best evidence available, inconclusive as it may be.

ILLUSTRATION OF THE DIFFICULTY OF CLEAR INFERENCE

Suppose we discovered an outbreak of strange psychological symptoms throughout the country. We might begin our efforts to understand the problem by interviewing some or all of the afflicted, with the aim of uncovering some common factor among them. Our interviews, let us say, suggest that all the people with the strange psychological symptoms had recently visited a physician and that they all had had prescribed for them a new drug whose side effects were not yet fully established. Now we suspect that the drug may, for some persons at least, be the determinant of the strange psychological symptoms. Shall we take a sample of people visiting physicians and arrange to give half of them the suspected drug? This would allow us to compare the two groups to see whether those given the drug were more likely to develop the strange psychological symptoms. But the ethical cost of such experimental research would be too high, for we would not be willing to expose people to a drug we had good reason to believe to be harmful.

As a practical alternative, we might want to compare those persons who were given the new drug by their physicians with those persons whose physicians did not prescribe the new drug. If only those given the drug developed the new symptoms, the drug would be more seriously implicated. But its determining role would still not be fully established. It might have been, for example, that those people given the new drug differed in some way from those who were not given the drug by their physicians. Not the new drug, but a correlate of being given the new drug could be the determining variable.

Other analyses are possible that might help us to judge whether the new drug is a determinant of the new symptoms. Among those patients given the drug some will very likely have been given large dosages while others will have been given small dosages. If it turns out that persons on larger dosages suffer more severely from the new symptoms, the drug will be more strongly implicated. However, we still cannot be certain about the causal role of the drug. It might be the case that those who were judged to be more ill by their physicians were given larger dosages, so that it is the illness for which the drug was prescribed that is the effective agent rather than the drug.

How have we satisfied Mill's three essentials for judging causes and effects? The first requirement was to show that the drug preceded the symptoms in time. Unless our medical records went back far enough, we would be unable to show that Y did not occur until after X. The second requirement was to show that taking the drug was related to the mysterious symptoms. Even if we could show that taking the drug was correlated with the mysterious symptoms, it might be argued that in order to be susceptible to the drug, a person had to be already in a given state of distress. It was not the drug, or *not only* the drug, that was related to the symptoms, according to this argument.

If we have not done very well in trying to satisfy Hume's basic requirements, it is even more difficult to rule out plausible rival hypotheses and thereby satisfy the third requirement. If the subjects who were in a state of distress were the only ones given the drug, then it is possible to explain the relationship by saying that the subjects were *self-selected* into the treatment group. Self-selection means that the subjects' state of distress was what determined the particular group in which they found themselves. What we seem to need is a comparison group of other subjects who were in a similar state of distress but were not given the drug.

Despite the difficulty of clear inference in this example, many scientists would probably be willing to be convinced by strong circumstantial, though inconclusive, evidence. Thus, if persons taking the drug were more likely to show the symptoms, if those taking more of the drug show more of the symptoms, and if those taking it over a longer period of time show more of the symptoms, a prudent scientist would be cautious about deciding that the drug *was not* a determinant of the symptoms. Even if an investigator were not willing to conclude that the drug was surely at the root of the symptoms, at least not on the basis of the type of evidence outlined, the researcher might well decide that it would be wisest to act as though it were.

SUMMARY

Behavioral scientists draw a distinction between independent and dependent variables. In the case of experimental research, independent variables are observable events that are manipulated in order to determine whether there is any effect upon another event (the dependent variable). While there are rules of logic for inferring the dependence of a variable, the nature of some relationships makes it difficult to draw conclusive or unequivocal causal inferences. In this case, taking into consideration the consequences of his or her decision, the scientist is sometimes willing to be convinced by circumstantial evidence even if the circumstances for demonstrating a determinative relationship are inconclusive. Whatever the variables in which the researcher is principally interested, it is essential that they be clearly defined in operational or theoretical terms in order for other scientists to understand exactly what is being studied.

KEY TERMS

cause and effect
dependent variable
determinative assertion
direction (as dependent variable)
ease (as dependent variable)
external (''pull'') independent variables
hypothetical construct
independent variable
internal (''push'') independent variables
operational definition
particularistic
persistence (as dependent variable)
requirements of causal inferences
self-selection of subjects
theoretical definition

CHAPTER 3

DESCRIBING, RELATING, AND EXPERIMENTING

Earlier we introduced the term "empirical" in connection with our discussion of the essential nature of the scientific method. We said that the scientific method is actually a misnomer, since it consists of many empirical methods rather than just one. We now turn to three prototypical empirical methods that are widely employed in behavioral research to study the what, when, and why of behavior. It is possible to distinguish two principal methods of scientific observation, the descriptive and the relational, and a special case of the second type, the experimental method. These three general types are not mutually exclusive, however; much research draws on aspects of more than one approach. The scope and logic of each of these types is the subject of this chapter.

THREE GENERAL METHODS OF INQUIRY

Descriptive research tends to have as its goal a careful mapping out of what happens behaviorally. The researcher who is interested in the study of children's failure in school may spend a good deal of time observing the classroom behavior of children who are doing poorly. The researcher can then describe as carefully as possible what was observed. Careful observation of failing pupils might lead to some revision of our concepts of classroom failure, to suggestions as to factors that may have contributed to the development of failure, and even perhaps to ideas for the remediation of failure.

The careful observation of behavior is a necessary first step in the development of a program of research in science, but it is rarely regarded as sufficient. Sooner or later someone will want to know *why* something happens behaviorally or *how* what happens behaviorally is related to other events. If our interest is in children's failure, we are not likely to be satisfied for very long with even the most careful description of that behavior. Sooner or later we will want to know the antecedents of failure and the outcomes of various procedures designed to reduce classroom failure. Even if we were not motivated directly by the practical implications of knowing the causes and cures of failure, we would believe our understanding of it to be considerably improved if we knew the conditions that increase and decrease its likelihood. To learn about the increase or decrease of failure behavior, or any other behavior, observations must focus on at least two variables at the same time. Two sets of observations must be made that can be related to one another.

This second case, *relational research* (often called "correlational research"), has as its goal the description of how what happens behaviorally changes along with changes in some other set of observations. Continuing with the classroom example, let us suppose that the researcher noted that many of the scholastically failing students were rarely looked at or addressed by their teachers and seldom exposed to new academically relevant information. At this stage the researcher might have only an impression about the relation between learning failure and teaching behavior. Such impressions of relationships are a frequent, and a frequently valuable, by-product of descriptive research. But if they are to be taken seriously as a relational principle, they cannot be left at the impressionistic level for very long. Our observer (or perhaps another observer who wanted to find out whether the first observer's impressions were accurate) might arrange to make a series of coordinated observations on a sample of pupils in classrooms that adequately represented the population of pupils about whom some conclusion was to be drawn. For each pupil it could be noted (*a*) whether the student was learning anything or the degree to which the student had been learning and (*b*) the degree to which the teacher had been exposing the student to material to be learned. From such coordinate observations, it should be possible to make a quantitative statement of the probable relationship between the amount of pupils' exposure to material to be learned and the amount of such material they did in fact learn.

To carry the illustration one step further, suppose that pupils exposed to less information were also those who tended to learn less. On discovering this relationship, there might be a temptation to conclude that children learn less because they are taught less. Such a hypothesis, while plausible, would not be warranted by the relationship reported. In this case, it might be that teachers teach less to those they know to be less able to learn. Differences in teaching behavior, then, may be as much a result of pupils' learning as a determinant of that learning. If we wanted to pursue our rival hypothesis, we could arrange to make further observations that would allow us to infer whether differences in information presented to pupils, apart from any individual differences among them, affected the pupils' learning. Such questions are best answered by manipulating the variables that one believes to be responsible for the effect.

This third case, *experimental research,* has as its goal the description of what happens behaviorally when something of interest to the experimenter is introduced into the situation. It permits answers to the question: "What leads to what?" Nonexperimental relational research can only rarely provide such information and then only under very special conditions. The difference between the strength of inference of nonexperimental and experimental observations can be expressed in the difference between the two statements "X is related to Y" and "X is responsible for Y." In our example, teaching is X and learning is Y. Our experiment is designed to reveal the effects of teaching on pupil learning. We might, therefore, select a sample of youngsters and, by tossing a coin or by means of some other random method, divide them into two equivalent groups. One of these groups would have more information given them by their teachers. The other group would be given less information. We could then assess which group of children's learning was superior. If the two groups differed, we would be in a position to ascribe the difference to the different treatments we had applied—more, compared to less, information.

There might still be a question of what it was about the better procedure that led to the improvement. In the case of increased teaching, for example, we might wonder whether the improvement was due to the additional material, the increased attention from the teacher while presenting the additional material, any accompanying increases in eye contact, smiles, warmth, or other possible correlates of increased teaching behavior. Each of these more-refined working hypotheses about the effective agents could be investigated in further studies involving descriptive and relational observations.

In fact, the amount of new material teachers present to their pupils is sometimes predictable not so much by the children's actual learning ability, but by their teachers' beliefs or expectations for the pupils' learning ability. It has been experimentally found that teachers' expectations about pupils' performance can come to serve as *self-fulfilling prophecies* (Rosenthal & Jacobson, 1968; Rosenthal & Rubin, 1978). That is to say, the occurrence of the expected behavior is caused by these very expectations.

DESCRIPTIVE RESEARCH: A PARADIGM CASE

To illustrate the richness of the descriptive, relational, and experimental approaches, we now turn to detailed cases of these three general types of research. All of the studies fall within the same area of behavioral science, specifically within the field of personality. The first study to be discussed was done under the auspices of the Office of Strategic Services (OSS), a World War II government agency in the United States charged with tasks such as intelligence gathering, sabotage behind enemy lines, mobilization of guerrilla groups to resist the Nazi occupation, and preparation and dissemination of propaganda (OSS Assessment Staff, 1948). We refer to this, and to the following, detailed models as *paradigm cases,* by which we mean that they represent classic or exemplary models of personality research.

The first paradigm case to be discussed concerns the program of assessment run by the OSS professional staff. Thousands of men, drawn from both military and civilian life, were recruited to carry out the often hazardous missions of the OSS. Initially it was not known what type of men to select for each of the various missions, and a group of psychologists and psychiatrists was assembled to aid in the assessment of the special agents. The chief contribution of these researchers was to set up a series of situations that would permit more useful and relevant descriptions of the personalities of the candidates. The original intent of the assessment staff had been more ambitious. It had been hoped that it would be possible to lower appreciably the error rate in the selection of recruits for the OSS and to increase the likelihood of assignment of agents to those missions they could best perform.

Unfortunately, several factors made the development of a screening and placement system that could be fairly and properly evaluated impossible. Chief among these factors were the assessment staff's not knowing what particular mission would finally be assigned to a recruit and, perhaps most importantly, several weaknesses in the final appraisal of how good a job an agent had actually done.

From December 1943 to August 1945, more than 5,000 recruits were studied by the assessment staff. The primary assessment station was located about an hour's ride from Washington, D.C., in a rustic setting of rolling meadows and stately trees. It was here that recruits were sent for a 3½-day period, during which they were given identical clothes to wear and assigned pseudonyms so that colonels and privates and college professors would be indistinguishable to the assessment personnel. Besides a false name, each recruit had to invent a cover story giving himself a new occupation, new residence, new place of birth, and a new educational background. Candidates were warned that the assessment staff would try to trick them into breaking cover and giving away their true identities.

Virtually everything that a recruit did from the moment he arrived at the station was observed and assessed: how he got off the truck that brought his group of recruits, the manner in which he asked questions of the staff members who explained procedures to the candidates, what he said at the first dinner, and what he chose to do after dinner when he was free to read or talk or withdraw. The first evening, candidates filled out a great many paper-and-pencil tests of personality and ability and also answered questions concerning personal background information.

The next few days were filled with many situational tests in which the staff had the opportunity to evaluate each man's level of initiative, leadership, functioning intelligence, social relationships, and physical ability. For example, in one situation a group of four to seven men had to move a log and a rock across an 8-foot-wide brook. The situation was rigged so that either a bridge or an overhead cable system could be constructed to solve the problem, but the achievement of a solution was not the main purpose of the exercise. Instead, it was to give the staff an opportunity to observe the different roles the men assumed in the team effort required to solve the problem.

One of the most trying, and possibly most revealing, situations was a task in which the candidates were to direct the efforts of two helpers in building a 5-foot cube out of a giant tinker-toy set.

Ostensibly the task was to assess the candidates' leadership ability. In actuality, it was a test of stress tolerance. "Kippy" and "Buster," the two helpers, were really two members of the assessment staff. Kippy was a passive sort who did nothing unless ordered to, except occasionally to get in the way. Buster offered useless suggestions, griped repeatedly, and harped on the candidates' weaknesses. Kippy and Buster together were sufficiently obstructive that, in the history of the OSS assessment program, no recruit was ever able to complete the task in the allotted 10 minutes.

Some of the candidates saw immediately that the two helpers were confederates; that insight sometimes, but not always, helped the candidates to contain their tempers and persist in trying to get the job done. Other candidates wondered why the OSS could not afford better farmhands around the estate and admitted that the obstreperousness and insolence of the helpers tempted them more than once to lay an uncharitable hand upon one or the other of them. On more than one occasion a fight did ensue. Some candidates learned enough about themselves from this experience that they asked to be excused from the program, realizing that the kind of stress involved would be too much for them.

During the candidates' half-week assessment period, they underwent many situational tests. It seems unlikely that, either before or since, so many people have been observed and described so carefully by so many experts in human behavior.

We have viewed the OSS project as a paradigm case of descriptive research, but it should be noted again that description had not been the only goal of the assessment staff. They had also hoped to correlate the assessment made of the men with their performance in the field, thereby using relational observation as well as descriptive research. Such correlations define the adequacy of the selection procedures, and when the correlations are high they tell that the *predictor variable* (in this case, the assessment) did its job of predicting the outcome or *criterion variable* (the actual job performance). Unfortunately, this type of relational outcome research had not been planned from the beginning, so there was no satisfactory evaluation of just how good a job had been done by the agents in the field. Even if such criterion information had been available, there is reason to suspect that the OSS assessment program could hardly have been very effective since the staff had only the vaguest (and probably sometimes erroneous) ideas about the nature of the jobs for which the candidates were being selected. It would be unreasonable indeed to think that one could select people for the performance of unspecified functions.

RELATIONAL RESEARCH: A PARADIGM CASE

The OSS assessment staff had been in a position to make many detailed observations relevant to many of the candidates' motives. However, there was not a planned, systematic attempt to relate the scores or ratings on any one of these variables to the scores or ratings on some subsequently measured variable that, on the basis of theory, should show a strong correlation with the predictor variable. In the field of personality research, there are, however, many studies that serve well to illustrate relational research. There are hundreds of studies showing how one personality attribute is related to some other personality attribute. For our next illustration, we shall discuss the development of a personality construct in which a means for its measurement was devised and then related to subjects' performance in a variety of other spheres as the construct would predict. By a *construct* we mean an abstract variable constructed from hypothetical ideas or images, which usually serves as an explanatory term that forms part of a theory.

At the very end of the 1950s, Douglas Crowne and David Marlowe, both of whom were at Ohio State University, set out to develop an instrument that would measure the *need for social approval* independent of the respondent's level of psychopathology. They began by considering hundreds of personality test items that were answered in a true-false format. To be included, an item had to be one that would reflect socially approved behavior but yet be almost certain to be untrue. In short, the items had to reflect behavior too good to be true. In addition, answers to the items could not have any implications of psychological abnormality or psychopathology. By having a group of psychology graduate students and faculty judge the social desirability of each item, and by having another group of psychology graduate students and faculty judge the degree of psychopathology implied by each item, it was possible to develop a set of items that would reflect behavior too virtuous to be probable, and that would simultaneously reflect no implication of personal maladjustment.

The final form of the test, called the Marlowe-Crowne Social-Desirability Scale, included 33 items (Crowne & Marlowe, 1964). In about half the items, a "true" answer reflected the socially desirable or higher need for approval response, and in about half the items, a "false" answer reflected the socially desirable response. An example of the former type of item might be: "I have never intensely disliked anyone," while an example of the latter might be: "I sometimes feel resentful when I don't get my way."

The items, combined to form a personality scale, showed a high degree of relationship with those measures with which the scale was expected to show high correlations. First, it correlated well with itself; that is, an impressive relationship was obtained between the two testings of a group of subjects who were tested one month apart. Thus the test seemed to be measuring what it measured in a *reliable* or consistent manner. In addition, though the test did show some moderate correlations with measures of psychopathology, there were fewer of these and they were smaller in magnitude than was the case for an earlier developed scale of social desirability. These were promising beginnings for the Marlowe-Crowne Scale, but it remained to be shown that the concept of need for social approval (and the scale developed to measure it) had a utility beyond predicting responses to other paper-and-pencil measures. As part of their program of further validating their new scale and the construct that was its basis, Crowne, Marlowe, and their students undertook an ingenious series of studies relating scores on their scale to subjects' behavior in a number of non-paper-and-pencil test situations.

In the first of these studies, subjects began by completing various tests, including the Marlowe-Crowne Scale, and then were asked to get down to the serious business of the experiment. This "serious business" required subjects to (a) pack a dozen spools of thread into a small box, (b) unpack the box, (c) repack the box, (d) re-unpack the box, and so on for 25 minutes while the experimenter appeared to be timing the performances and making notes about them. After these dull 25 minutes had elapsed, subjects were asked to rate how interesting the task had been, how instructive, how important to science, and how much the subject wanted to participate in similar experiments in the future. The results of this study showed quite clearly that those subjects who scored above the mean on need for approval said that they found the task more interesting, more instructive, more important to science, and that they were more eager to participate again in similar studies than those subjects who had scored below the mean. Apparently then, just as we would have predicted, subjects higher in the need for social approval said nicer things to their high-status experimenter about the task that he had set for them.

Next, the investigators conducted a series of studies employing the method of verbal conditioning. In one variation of this procedure, the subject is asked to say all the words he or she can think of to the listening experimenter. In the positive reinforcement condition, every time the subject utters a plural noun the experimenter responds affirmatively by saying "Mm-hmm." In the negative reinforcement condition, every time the subject utters a plural noun, the experimenter responds negatively by saying "Uh-uh." In these procedures, the magnitude of verbal conditioning is usually defined by the increase in the production of plural nouns from the prereinforcement level to some subsequent time block after the subject has received the reinforcements. Magnitude of verbal conditioning is often thought to be a good index of a simple type of susceptibility to social influence. Subjects who are more susceptible to the experimenter's reinforcements are thought to be also more susceptible to other forms of elementary social influence.

In the first of their verbal conditioning studies, the investigators found that subjects higher in the need for social approval responded with far more plural nouns when positively reinforced than did subjects lower in the need for approval. Similarly, subjects higher in need for approval responded with fewer plural nouns when negatively reinforced than did subjects lower in the need for social approval. In this particular study, those subjects who saw the connection between their utterances and the experimenter's reinforcement were dropped. In this way, the relationship obtained was between subjects' need for approval as measured by the Marlowe-Crowne Scale and subjects' responsivity to the approval of their experimenter but only when they were not explicitly aware (or said they were unaware) of the role of the experimenter's reinforcement.

In the second of their verbal conditioning studies, the investigators wanted to employ a task that would be more lifelike and more engaging than producing random words. For this purpose, subjects were asked to describe their own personality and every positive self-reference was reinforced by the experimenter's saying "Mm-hmm" in a flat monotone. A positive self-reference was defined as any statement reflecting favorably upon the subject and, despite this seemingly vague definition, two judges working independently showed a very high degree of consistency in identifying positive self-references. Results of this study showed that subjects above the mean in need for social approval made significantly more positive self-references when reinforced for doing so than did subjects scoring lower in the need for approval. It now appeared that regardless of whether the subjects' responses were as trivial as the production of random words or as meaningful as talking about themselves, these responses could be increased much more by subtle social reinforcement if the subjects were higher in their measured need for social approval.

In their third verbal conditioning study, the investigators employed a vicarious reinforcement method. In this procedure, the subject was not reinforced for a given type of response, but instead watched someone else receive reinforcement. The real subjects of the study observed a *pseudosubject*, a confederate of the experimenter, make up a series of sentences using one of six pronouns and a verb given by the experimenter. Whenever the pseudosubject began his sentence with the pronouns "I" or "We," the experimenter said the word "good." Before and after the observation period, subjects themselves made up sentences using one of the same six pronouns. Results of the study showed that subjects higher in need for approval showed a significantly greater increase in their use of "I" and "We" from their pre-observational to their postobservational sentence-construction session than did subjects lower in the need for social approval. Thus, once again it was shown that subjects can be successfully predicted to be more responsive to the approving behavior of an experimenter when they have scored higher on a test of the need for approval.

Still another set of studies was undertaken to extend the validity of the Marlowe-Crowne Scale and of the construct of need for approval. This time the procedure employed was a derivative of a conformity procedure developed by social psychologist Solomon Asch (1952). In this situation, a group of subjects was required to make judgments on specific issues. Judgments were announced by each subject, and the purpose of the technique was to permit an assessment of the effects of earlier subjects' judgments on the judgments of subsequent judges. In order to control the judgments made earlier, accomplices were employed to play the role of subjects, and these pseudosubjects were instructed to make the same judgment, one that was quite clearly in error. Conformity was defined as the real subject's "going along with" (conforming to) the majority in his or her own judgment rather than giving the objectively correct response.

In one of Marlowe and Crowne's variations on this procedure, the subjects listened to a tape recording of knocks on a table and then reported their judgment of the number of knocks they had heard. Each subject was led to believe she was the fourth subject, and she heard the tape-recorded responses of three prior subjects to each series of knocks that were to be judged. The earlier three subjects were, of course, pseudosubjects, and they all agreed with one another by consistently giving an incorrect response on 12 of the 18 trials. For each real subject, then, it was possible to count the number of times out of 12 that she yielded to the wrong but unanimous majority. Results showed that subjects scoring higher in the need for social approval did indeed conform more to the majority judgment than subjects scoring lower in the need for approval.

In the Asch-type situation employed, the wrong but unanimous majority had not been physically present in the room with the subjects, and the investigators wanted to know whether they would obtain the same results employing "live" accomplices. This time the task was a discrimination problem in which subjects had to judge which of two clusters of dots was larger. Once again, pseudosubjects were employed to give responses that were clearly wrong but that were unanimous. As before, the results showed that subjects scoring above the mean on the need for approval measure yielded more often to the unanimous but erring majority than did the subjects scoring below the mean.

We have now seen a substantial number of studies that support the *validity* of the Marlowe-Crowne Scale (the fact that it measures what it purports to measure) and document the utility of their concept of the need for social approval. There are studies, to be sure, that do not support the investigators' major findings, but there are also additional findings that do. Our purpose here is not to be exhaustive, but to document an unusually elegant series of studies that serves well to illustrate the nature of relational research in one area of behavioral science.

EXPERIMENTAL RESEARCH: A PARADIGM CASE

We usually speak of "experimental research" when the investigator has introduced a new feature into the environment for some of the research subjects and then has compared the reactions of these subjects with the reactions of other subjects who have not been exposed to the new feature. In both the OSS program and in the Crowne and Marlowe research on need for approval, there were many instances in which the investigators introduced some new feature, some experimental manipulation, into the situation. Yet, we did not regard those manipulations as exemplifying experimental research because "comparison" was not the primary interest, that is, a comparison between the behavior of subjects exposed to the new feature and the behavior of subjects not exposed to the new feature. We now turn to another example from the field of personality research to illustrate the experimental approach, the research of Harry and Margaret Harlow and their coworkers dealing with affection in primates.

There are few personality theories that do not consider early life experiences to be of special importance in the development of personality. Among the early life experiences often given special attention are those involving mother-child relationships. A generally posed proposition might be this one: loving mother-child relationships are more likely to lead to healthy adult personalities than hostile, rejecting mother-child relationships. To investigate this hypothesis experimentally, we would be required to assign half our sample of young children to loving mothers and half to rejecting mothers and follow up the development of each child's adult personality. Such an experimental plan is an ethical absurdity in our culture's value matrix, although there are no special problems of experimental logic involved. Does this mean that behavioral scientists can never do experimental work on important questions of human development and human personality? One approach to the problem has capitalized on the biological continuities between nonhuman organisms and human beings. Primates especially have been shown to share attributes with humans sufficiently to make them valuable, if far from exact or even very accurate, models for humankind. We cannot, for the sake of furthering our knowledge of personality development, separate a human baby from its mother, but the important lessons we might learn from such separation make it seem rational, if not easily (or readily) justifiable, to separate a nonhuman primate from its mother.

In their extensive research program at the University of Wisconsin, the Harlows and their collaborators employed an array of research procedures and approaches of both the psychologist and the biologist. Much of their research on the affectional system of monkeys was of the descriptive type (e.g., young monkeys become attached to other young monkeys) and of the relational type (e.g., male monkeys become more forceful with age; female monkeys become more passive). Our interest here, however, will focus on their experimental research although we shall be able to describe only a fraction of it.

As part of that research program, infant monkeys were separated from their mothers just a few hours after birth and were raised by bottle with great success. The Harlows had been advised by Dr. Gertrude van Wagenen to have available for their infant monkeys some soft pliant surfaces, and folded gauze diapers were consequently made available to all the baby monkeys. The babies became very much attached to these diapers, so much so that they could only be removed for laundering with great difficulty. These observations led to an experiment designed so that it would show more systematically the shorter- and longer-term effects of access to a soft material. The research was planned also to shed light on the question of the relative importance to the development of the infant's attachment to its mother of being fed by her as opposed to being in close and cuddly contact with her (Harlow, 1959, 1966).

Accordingly two "pseudomothers" were built: one a bare, welded-wire cylindrical form with a crude wooden head and face attached, the other a similar apparatus covered with terry cloth. Eight newborn monkeys were given equal access to the wire-and-cloth mother figures, but four of the monkeys were fed at the breast of the wire mother, and four were fed at the breast of the cloth mother. Results showed that when the measures were of the amount of milk consumed or the amount of weight gained, the two mothers made no difference. The monkeys fed by the two mothers drank about the same amount of milk and gained about the same amount of weight. However, regardless of which mother had fed them, baby monkeys spent much more time climbing up on the cloth mother and clinging to her than they did on the wire mother. This finding was important for a number of reasons; not only for demonstrating the importance of contact comfort but also for showing that a simple earlier formulation of love for mother was really much too simple. That earlier formulation held that mothers became prized because they were associated with the reduction of hunger and thirst. The Harlow results show quite clearly that being the source of food is not nearly as good a predictor of a baby's subsequent preference as is being a soft and cuddly mother. When the monkeys were about 100 days old, they spent an average of about 15 hours a day on the cloth mother but only about 1.5 hours on the wire mother, regardless of whether it had been the cloth or wire mother that had fed the baby monkey.

Later experiments showed that when the infant monkey was placed into a fear-arousing situation, it was the cloth mother that was sought out for comfort and reassurance. A frightened monkey, confronted by a mechanical bear that advanced while beating a drum, would flee to the cloth mother, secure a dose of reassurance, then gradually explore the frightening objects and begin to turn them into toys. When the cloth mother was not in the room, the infant monkeys hurled themselves onto the floor, clutched their heads and bodies, and screamed in distress. The bare-wire mother provided the infant with no greater security or reassurance than did no mother at all.

A collaborator in the Harlow group, Robert A. Butler, had discovered that monkeys enclosed in a dimly lit box would spend hour after hour pressing a lever that would open a window in the box and give them a chance to see something outside. Monkeys barely able to walk will press the lever for a brief peek at the world outside. One of the variables that determines how hard the monkey will work to look out the window is what there is to be seen. When the monkey infants we have been discussing were tested in the "Butler box," it turned out that monkeys worked as hard to see their cloth mothers as to see another real monkey. On the other hand, they worked no harder to see the wire mother than to see nothing at all outside the box. Not only in this experiment, but to a surprising degree in general, a wire mother is not much better than no mother at all, but a cloth mother comes close to being as good as the real thing. (The Harlows have, however, found other views prevalent among monkey fathers.)

A number of female monkeys became mothers themselves although they had not had any monkey mothers of their own and no physical contact with age-mates during the first year of their life (Harlow & Harlow, 1965). Compared to normal monkey mothers, these unmothered mothers were usually brutal to their firstborn offspring, hitting them, kicking them, and crushing them. Those motherless mothers who were not brutal were indifferent. The most cheerful result of this experiment was that those motherless monkeys who went on to become mothers for a second time, treated their second babies in a normal or even an overprotective manner.

A very important series of studies required that infant monkeys be raised in social isolation (Harlow & Harlow, 1970). When the isolation is total, the young monkey is exposed to no other living animals or humans; all its physical needs are met in automated fashion. A major independent variable is length of isolation since birth: 0, 3, 6, or 12 months. All the monkeys raised in isolation were physically healthy, but when placed into a new environment they appeared to crouch in terror. Those monkeys that had been isolated only 3 months recovered from their neurotic fear within a month or so. Those monkeys that had been isolated for 6 months never did quite recover. Their play behavior, even after 6 months, was minimal and isolated. Their social activity, when it did occur, was directed only to monkeys that had also been raised in isolation. Those monkeys that had been isolated for 12 months showed the most severe retardation of play and of the development of aggression. Apathetic and terrified, these monkeys were defenseless against the attacks of the healthy control group monkeys.

Longer-term effects of early social isolation have also been discovered. Several years later, the 6-months-isolated monkeys showed a dramatic change in orientation to other monkeys. Whereas earlier they had been attacked by other monkeys and had not bothered to defend themselves, they had by now developed into pathological aggressors, attacking other monkeys large and small, acts virtually never occurring among normal monkeys of their age. Another long-term effect of early social isolation can be seen in the inadequacy of the sexual behavior of these monkeys. Even females who were only partially isolated in infancy avoid contact with breeding males, do not groom themselves, engage in threats, in aggression, in clutching themselves, biting themselves, and failing often to support the male should mounting occur. Normal females rarely engage in any of these behaviors. Male monkeys who have been isolated show even more serious sexual inadequacy than do the isolated females. When contrasted with normal males, they groom less, threaten more, are more aggressive, initiate little sex contact, engage in unusual sex behavior, and almost never achieve intromission.

In the extensive research program of the Harlow group, there were many other experiments. Some monkeys were raised without mothers but with access to age-mates while other monkeys were raised by their mothers but without access to age-mates (Harlow & Harlow, 1966). The overall results, while complicated, suggested that both normal mothering and normal age-mate contact are important to normal social development but that to some extent each can substitute for some deficits in the other. Both types of experience are better than either alone, but either alone appears to be very much better than neither.

SUMMARY

We have looked at hypothetical and actual examples of descriptive, relational, and experimental research in behavioral science. Descriptive research tells "how things are," but can also carry implications of relationships. Relational research tells "how things are in relation to other things" and thus reveals what variables are associated or correlated. Experimental research, by manipulating specific independent variables, tells "how things get to be the way they are." When the same question can be answered by experimental and nonexperimental means, behavioral scientists usually prefer to do experiments because of the greater strength of causal inference that is generally associated with the experimental approach. But (as we also saw in Chapter 2) researchers do not always have this option open to them, and they conduct research of a descriptive or relational nature because that may be all they can conduct. Sometimes, to be sure, they conduct nonexperimental research because that is what seems most urgently needed at that stage of their knowledge in a given area.

KEY TERMS

construct
criterion variable
descriptive research
experimental research
need for social approval
paradigm case
predictor variable
pseudosubject
relational research
self-fulfilling prophecy
validity

HYPOTHESIS TESTING

CHAPTER 4

REFUTATION AND CORROBORATION

"Take pencil and paper; carefully observe, and write down what you have observed!" This is all the eminent philosopher Karl Popper once told some students of his. They, of course, immediately responded by asking *what* it was he wanted them to observe, since observation needs a chosen object, a definite task, an interest, a point of view, and a problem. Scientific observation is no exception, and the scientist's hypothesis or theory selects what is to be observed. But not every hypothesis or theory is scientific. As Popper has pointed out, only those hypotheses and theories that are potentially *refutable*, no matter how speculative, are considered scientific (Popper, 1934, 1963). The philosophy behind this assertion, which forms the basis of the logic of scientific corroboration, is the focal point of this chapter.

WHAT IS HYPOTHESIS TESTING?

Suppose you were walking along the street and a shady character approached and whispered that he had a quarter to sell for only five dollars. He claimed that this was a quarter with some extraordinary properties. When properly used, this quarter could win you fame and fortune, because it would not always come up heads and tails with equal regularity. Instead, one outcome was more likely than the other. A smart bettor could, when flipping the coin, simply predict the alternative that occurred most frequently.

If the claim about the quarter were true, you might want to own it. You would want to know two things before you bought it: (*a*) Is the coin really ''not fair''? (that is, is the probability of flipping a head not equal to the probability of flipping a tail?) and (*b*) Is the difference between the probability of flipping a head sufficiently different from one in two to make it worth your while?

You must test the hypothesis that the probability of heads equals the probability of tails. You flip a coin once and a head appears. The shady character says, ''There, I told you, it almost always comes up heads.'' You flip the coin again, and again it comes up heads. Suppose you flipped the coin 10 times and each time it came up heads. Would you believe the character at this point? If you answered ''yes,'' then would you have believed him if after 10 tosses there were nine heads and one tail? This is the essential question in hypothesis testing. We can be as stringent as we like in setting rejection criteria, but we may eventually pay for this decision by rejecting what we perhaps should not. Before we state more precisely the ideas involved in this process, let us first see how Karl Popper understands the refutation and corroboration of scientific theories and the hypotheses derived from them.

RISKY PREDICTIONS AND THE PRINCIPLE OF FALSIFIABILITY

As noted previously, the criterion of the scientific status of theories is their refutability or *falsifiability,* in Popper's terms. Thus a theory that is not refutable by any conceivable event is considered nonscientific. Let us suppose it were theorized that human beings are direct descendants of extraterrestrial creatures who, thousands of years ago, arrived in flying saucers to colonize Earth. The problem with this theory, from a scientific point of view, is that it is not refutable by any conceivable event. On the other hand, it should be relatively easy for a fertile imagination to uncover or fabricate all sorts of vague ''data'' to confirm the previously earthly existence of intelligent creatures from outer space. In science, confirmations count only if they are the result of *risky predictions*, which is to say, refutable hypotheses.

Just how easy it is to find confirmations for nearly every theory, if a person looks hard enough, can be illustrated by a classic example from the annals of psychiatry, Mesmer's ''animal magnetism theory.'' Franz Anton Mesmer, an eighteenth-century Viennese physician, observed that patients who touched a magnetized wand or tube during a seance immediately fell into a trancelike sleep. Theorizing that somehow an invisible "fluid" had rearranged parts of their brains, he further hypothesized that a "magnetic current" was the basis of this mysterious phenomenon. He was treating a young female patient, nicknamed "Franzl," who was suffering from a form of hysteria (fainting, temporary paralysis, agonizing aches and pains, etc.), and he thought the magnetic cure was worth trying on her nervous disorder. From observing the periodicity of her attacks, he theorized that it should be possible to stem their ebb and flow by having her swallow a preparation containing iron and then placing magnets of assorted shapes and sizes on parts of her body. He found that by turning the "magnetic currents" in different directions, he could control Franzl's symptoms and actually cure her for several hours at a time (Buranelli, 1975).

It seems that everywhere Mesmer looked he found confirmations for his magnetic current theory. Ernest R. Hilgard (1980), in his introduction to Mesmer's writings, reminds us that Mesmer accumulated evidence that *something* was happening even though his theory was far-fetched by modern standards. What Mesmer had found, of course, was the precursor of hypnosis and the powerful effect of suggestibility. Indeed he soon found that he could produce the same effects without the use of actual magnets, even when he applied objects made of cloth or wood. They became "magnetized" because he, Mesmer, had touched them, he concluded. *He* was the "animal magnet"! One patient who had suffered hearing loss during a thunderstorm was miraculously cured when Mesmer held his hands over the patient's ears. Another patient lost his stomach ache when Mesmer gently stroked away the spasms.

Eventually circumstances caught up with Mesmer, in the form of a blue-ribbon commission which investigated his medical claims. For reasons not entirely clear, he left Vienna to establish a practice in Paris in 1778. To the French scientists, his magnetic cure seemed preposterous, and a scientific commission (including the American diplomat Benjamin Franklin) was organized to look into them. The commission's rejection of Mesmer's medical claims eventually led to his downfall, although in his frustration he formed a secret society of disciples, known as the Society of Harmony, to try again to propagate the faith in animal magnetism.

STUBBORN THEORIES: AN EXAMPLE

We have said that it is not the verifiability, but the falsifiability, of a theory (or hypothesis) that is considered essential in science. If one theory, T′, is more falsifiable than another theory, T, and if

T' has survived more severe testing than has T, it follows that T' must be a better scientific theory than T (Popper, 1963).

Theories are stubborn, however, and even some genuinely scientific theories, when specific hypotheses are found to be false, are still upheld by their admirers by reinterpreting the theory in such a way that escapes refutation (Popper, 1963). A recent example would be Leon Festinger's theory of cognitive dissonance (Festinger, 1957). Festinger, in trying to account for the fact that some earthquake survivors in India spread rumors about future catastrophes instead of seeking gratification in fantasy, was inspired to develop two important hypotheses that became the starting point for an elaborate program of experimental investigation.

Festinger wondered why those rumors arose and were so widely accepted, since the belief that terrible disasters are coming seems frightening. He theorized that there should be "cognitive dissonance" arising from the experience of having survived a devastating earthquake in which others had perished. The rumors, he reasoned, gave the survivors something to be frightened *about*—and this was reassuring for them in a way! That is, since the rumors provided them with information that jibed with the way they already felt, the rumors were anxiety justifying and dissonance reducing instead of anxiety provoking, he theorized. On the basis of this interpretation, he developed two interrelated propositions to explain why individuals strive for psychological consistency (or consonance) when they are experiencing, or expect to experience, *cognitive dissonance* (defined as inconsistent knowledge, opinions, or beliefs about the environment). One proposition was that this dissonance, being psychologically uncomfortable, will motivate the person to reduce the dissonance and achieve consonance. The second proposition was that when this dissonance is present, besides trying to reduce it, the person will try to avoid situations and information that might increase the dissonance.

These and other propositions of cognitive dissonance theory have been carefully scrutinized by many scientists. The results of several empirical investigations have actually tended to refute one or two core propositions of Festinger's theory. Nevertheless, cognitive dissonance theory has survived, and continues to thrive, as its advocates have introduced *ad hoc* assumptions to assure that it escapes refutation. As a consequence, its area of application is now more restricted. Indeed some of the studies originally discussed by Festinger no longer even apply. For instance, it is now theorized that being responsible for one's actions is essential for dissonance reduction to occur. However, earthquake survivors would not *feel responsible* for surviving, since the earthquake was a surprise to them and a natural occurrence beyond their control. Thus this central study, which Festinger originally used as a point of departure in developing his theory, no longer pertains to his rearticulated theory (Greenwald & Ronis, 1978).

NULL HYPOTHESES AND THE TWO TYPES OF ERROR

In spite of Popper's claim that there is such a thing as a completely decisive falsifying test of a theory, others have argued that when a refutation occurs this merely tells the scientist that the theory needs to be modified, not that it needs to be discarded. They might point to the evolution of cognitive dissonance theory as a recent example to illustrate this counterargument to Popper's position. Nevertheless, most researchers seem to proceed as if the ideal of a completely decisive falsifying test was a reality. All they usually ask is whether the conclusions they reach (or wish to reach) can be justified on the basis of *significance testing*.

Significance testing refers to the statistical evaluation of what are called "null hypotheses." Its purpose is to allow researchers to draw conclusions about the "truth value" of their theories in as precise a quantitative fashion and as objective a manner as possible. As we shall see in a moment, significance testing is not the only aid available to the researcher for evaluating a set of conclusions. But it has traditionally carried most of the weight of scientific inference in many areas of behavioral science.

To understand the logic of the statistical evaluation of null hypotheses, we must understand not only what a null hypothesis is but also the two basic errors of inference that concern researchers, the type I error and the type II error. The *null hypothesis* is simply one that entertains the possibility that there is no relationship between the variables under investigation. Suppose the experimenter's working hypothesis claimed that "jogging makes you feel better" or that "similarity leads to attraction"; the null hypothesis would state the counterclaim that "jogging does *not* make you feel better" or that "similarity does *not* lead to attraction." The *type I error* (or "error of the first kind") consists of claiming a relationship that does not exist, and the *type II error* (or "error of the second kind") consists of failing to claim a relationship that does exist.

To illustrate, let us return to the shady character who was peddling a quarter for five dollars. Suppose you initially hypothesize that the quarter is fair. In other words, you are hypothesizing that the probability of heads equals the probability of tails—this would be the null hypothesis. You would then match this with an alternative one, which is that the coin is not fair; that is, the probability of heads is not equal to the probability of tails. You now test these two possibilities by performing an "experiment" to determine which hypothesis you cannot reject. To make such a decisive test the two possibilities must be *mutually exclusive* (when one is true the other must be false). Table 4.1 summarizes these ideas and shows how your decision might lead to a type I error, a type II error, or no error, depending on what your conclusion was and what the actual state of affairs was. This example also points out that the type I error represents an error of "gullibility" or "overeagerness," and the type II an error of "conservatism" or "blindness to a relationship."

The probability of the type I error is symbolized as *alpha* (α), and the probability of the type II error is symbolized as *beta* (β). Another name for *alpha* is the *significance level*. Thus when researchers do "significance testing" they are asking the question: "What is the probability of the type I error?" This does not mean that they are indifferent to the probability of committing the type II error, but the fact is that they do usually attach a greater psychological importance to errors of the first kind. Put another way, when researchers do significance testing they are trying to state precisely the significance level to be more sure that they

TABLE 4.1
EXAMPLE TO ILLUSTRATE DEFINITIONS OF TYPE I AND II ERRORS

	Actual state of affairs	
Your decision	The coin is fair	The coin is not fair
The coin is not fair (i.e., it can win you fame and fortune since it will not come up heads and tails equally).	Type I error ("gullibility")	No error
The coin is fair (i.e., it cannot win you fame and fortune since it is an ordinary coin).	No error	Type II error ("blindness")

have not accepted a falsehood. In theory, then, the behavioral scientist attaches a greater loss to accepting a falsehood (type I error) than to failing to acknowledge a truth (type II error). This habit of being conservative in one's judgment is sometimes explained (some might say rationalized) as the "healthy skepticism characteristic of the scientific temper" (cf. Axinn, 1966; Kaplan, 1964).

Table 4.2 recasts what we have said so far into a matrix showing the various implications of the scientist's decision to reject or not to reject the null hypothesis. Previously we mentioned that significance testing is not the only aid available for reaching a decision, and we now turn to a related procedure known as *power analysis*.

POWER ANALYSIS AS AN AID TO SIGNIFICANCE TESTING

Power analysis is most usefully regarded as a complementary aid to be used together with significance testing. *Power* can be defined as the probability of rejecting the null hypothesis when the null hypothesis is false and in need of rejecting. Power increases as the probability of the type II error (*beta*) decreases, that is,

$$\text{Power} = 1 - \text{beta}$$

Put another way, power is the probability of *not* making a type II error.

Two major purposes of power analysis are (*a*) the planning of research and (*b*) the evaluation of research already completed. In

TABLE 4.2
IMPLICATIONS OF THE DECISION TO REJECT OR NOT TO REJECT THE NULL HYPOTHESIS

Scientist's decision	Actual state of affairs	
	Null hypothesis is true	**Null hypothesis is false**
Reject null hypothesis	Type I error (claiming a relationship that does not exist)	No decision error
Do not reject null hypothesis	No decision error	Type II error (failing to claim a relationship that does exist)

the planning of research, a power analysis is conducted to determine the size of the sample needed to reach a given alpha level for any particular size of effect that might be expected. Size of effect (or *effect size*) refers to the degree to which the relationship studied differs from zero. In the evaluation of completed research and its accompanying inferences, scientists employ a power analysis to help them decide whether a given failure to detect an effect at a given alpha was likely to have been due primarily to the employment of too small a sample. The reason for this is that the larger the sample size or number of observations, the easier it is to detect an effect at a given alpha.

Let us consider an example (one to which we return in a later chapter). Smith conducts an experiment on the effects of her treatment of learning disabilities by randomly assigning 40 children to the manipulation (or *experimental*) condition and 40 children to the nonmanipulation (or *control*) condition. Smith reports that the experimental condition children improved significantly more than the control condition children at an alpha less than one in 20. This means that there is less than one chance in 20 of having mistakenly rejected the null hypothesis. Jones is skeptical and decides to check on Smith's results by assigning children at random to the same two conditions. Jones has 20 children available for the research, and he assigns 10 to each condition. His results show alpha actually greater than three in 10. Jones publishes his findings, claiming Smith's results were *unreplicable* (not repeatable) and not to be believed.

Consumers of research relying on alpha levels alone to tell them whether the research had been replicated or not might be seriously misled by Jones's conclusions of nonreplication. As we shall see in a later discussion, a closer look at Jones's data would show not only that Jones's results were in the same direction as Smith's, but more importantly, that Jones's effect size was exactly the same as Smith's. In short, the two experiments showed the *same* effect! But Smith's sample size was large enough to show an effect at alpha less than one in 20, while Jones's sample size was not large enough to show the effect even at alpha less than three in 10.

In a given study, the determination of the level of power at which the scientist would be operating depends on several factors. It depends on the particular statistic the scientist employs to determine the significance level and on the level of significance (alpha) selected. It also depends on the size of the sample employed and on the size of the effect the scientist is studying. We

return to the question of effect size in later discussions when we
also examine the specifics of significance testing.

SUMMARY

Scientific corroboration consists of submitting risky predictions
to empirical testing. However, even genuinely scientific theories
can be reinterpreted so as to escape refutation. Nevertheless,
most behavioral scientists proceed from the ideal (if not the
reality) of Popper's falsification thesis, and they employ significance testing in making a decision about the tenability of the null
hypothesis. Researchers relying on significance testing alone can
be misled, which is why more and more researchers are estimating effect sizes as well. Whereas investigators typically have considered only the risk of type I errors they are increasingly also
considering the risk of type II errors. This latter type of risk is
examined by means of a power analysis.

KEY TERMS

alpha (α)
beta (β)
control condition
effect size
experimental condition
falsifiability
mutually exclusive
null hypothesis
power = 1 − beta
power analysis
refutability
risky prediction
significance level (alpha)
significance testing (hypothesis testing)
theory
type I and II errors

CHAPTER 5

THE LOGIC OF CONTROL

The concept of *control* is central to all of the sciences. Derived from "counter-roll," it originally referred to a master list used to check and correct other lists. In behavioral science, there are four distinct usages of control: constancy of conditions, control series, behavior control, and the control group (Boring, 1969). We begin by differentiating these common usages. We then focus on the fourth meaning, which is most closely and specifically tied to the logic of experimental design.

FOUR COMMON USAGES

1 *Constancy of conditions* refers to the importance of controlling or maintaining those conditions that affect the variables of the research at those levels or values at which the scientist wants them or at which the scientist believes them to be. Scientists might at some future time want to study the effect of temperature variation on behavior under controlled conditions. But unless that were the objective, it would not be good scientific practice to allow the temperature in the laboratory to vary capriciously from very chilly to very hot under uncontrolled conditions. If that occurs, the scientist would not be able to claim the constancy of conditions that allows statements of relationships to be made confidently. In this case, the scientist controls the ambient temperature by holding it constant in order to eliminate the possibility that it can introduce error into the research findings and thus produce spurious results.

2 *Control series* refers to the calibration of various elements of the research, including in some cases the apparatus used or even the research participants' mental set. For example, in psychophysical research, the subjects may be asked to judge whether their skin is being touched by one or two fine compass points. If subjects know that two points will always be applied, they may never report the sensation of being stimulated by only one point. Yet it is known that when two points are sufficiently close to one another they are invariably perceived as only one point. A control series might consist of applying only one point on a certain percentage of the trials. If the subjects do not know when they are receiving one or two points, their responses are less likely to be influenced by the power of suggestion (by their expectation of what they are receiving).

3 *Behavior control* pertains to the manipulation or shaping of behavior based on a particular schedule of reinforcement. Behaviorists, such as B. F. Skinner, have used this term to denote the manipulation of the environmental conditions to which organisms are exposed in order to bring about a definite behavioral outcome. Behavior control is thus generally used to refer to an organism's dependency on obtaining rewards by acting in certain ways.

4 *Control group* typically refers to the use of a condition against which scientists compare the effects of the experimental condition. The story is told of how the ancient Egyptians used a control group to discover that citron is an antidote for poison (Jones, 1964). It seems that a magistrate had sentenced some convicted criminals to be executed by exposing them to poisonous snakes. It was reported to him, however, that none of the criminals had died despite the fact that his sentence had been carried out with extreme care. Inquiring into the matter, he learned that the criminals, just before they were bitten by the snakes, had been given some citron to eat by an old woman who took pity on them. The magistrate surmised that the citron had saved them, and he had the criminals divided into pairs in order to test his hypothesis. Citron was fed to one of each pair and not to the other. When the criminals were again exposed to the poisonous snakes, the criminals who had eaten the citron suffered no harm while the untreated controls died instantly. This grisly story illustrates an early use of control groups.

MILL'S "JOINT METHOD" OF CONDITIONS

That fourth sense of the term also embodies some ideas subsequently developed by John Stuart Mill. We mentioned Mill's name in Chapter 2, in connection with his logical rules for unraveling causes and effects. Mill also established other principles which later became the foundation for statistical procedures in experimental design.

One of three such principles is the *method of agreement;* it states: "If X, then Y." The statement means that whenever X occurs, Y automatically follows. When this happens, X and Y are related in the sense that one follows the other. It also means that X is a *sufficient condition* of Y, which tells us that X is adequate for the occurrence of Y.

A second principle of Mill's is the *method of difference*; it states: "If not-X, then not-Y." In other words, when X is not present, Y does not occur. This means that X is a *necessary condition* of Y, that is to say, X is requisite or essential for the occurrence of Y.

Putting these two principles together, we have a third principle called the *joint method of agreement and difference* (or simply the "joint method"). It states "If X, then Y" *and* "If not-X, then not-Y." The joint method informs us that X is both necessary and sufficient for the occurrence of Y.

EXPERIMENTAL AND CONTROL GROUPS IN PRACTICE

Let us imagine that X represents a new and highly touted tranquilizer that can be obtained without prescription, while Y represents a decrease in measured tension. Say that we have a group of subjects who complain of tension, that they take a certain dosage of the tranquilizer, and then show a reduction in tension. What we have described so far is a standard experimental group in which X occurred and then Y occurred. But could we conclude from this single observation that it was the tranquilizer that led to the reduction in tension?

Not yet, since we have established only that X is a sufficient condition of Y. What we require is a control group against which to compare the reaction in the experimental group. For our control, let us suppose we have a group of comparable subjects who were not given any pills, and that they did not show any tension reduction. In other words, when X did not occur, then Y also did not occur. We can diagram this two-group design as follows, and we quickly see that it corresponds to Mill's joint method:

Experimental group	Control group
If *X*, then *Y*	If not-*X*, then not-*Y*

Could we now conclude that taking the drug is what led to tension reduction? Yes, but with the stipulation that "taking the drug" means something quite different from getting a certain chemical into the blood system. "Taking the drug" means among other things: (*a*) having someone give the subject a pill; (*b*) having someone give the subject the attention that goes with pill giving; (*c*) having the subject believe that relevant medication has been administered; and (*d*) having the ingredients of the drug find their way to the blood system of the subject.

Usually when testing a new drug the researcher is interested only in the subject's physical reaction to active ingredients. The researcher does not care to learn that subjects will get to feeling better if they believe they are being helped, because this fact is already established. But if the researcher knows this, then how is it possible to separate the effects of the drug's ingredients from the effects of pill giving, subject expectations of help, and other psychological variables that may also be sufficient conditions of *Y*? The answer is by the choice of a different or an additional control group.

This time we will employ not a group given nothing, but instead a group given something that differs only in terms of the ingredients whose effects we would like to establish. The need for this type of control is so well established in drug research that virtually all trained investigators routinely use *placebo-control groups*—a placebo is a substance without any pharmacological effect but given as a "drug" to a control group. (The general finding, incidentally, is that placebos are often effective, and sometimes even *as* effective as the far more expensive drug for which they serve as the relevant control.)

In this research, the scientist first employed a no-pill control group and then a placebo, or "sugar pill," control group. Assuming that there is often a choice of control groups, how does the scientist decide on the most appropriate control group? This question is not a simple one, but two of the major factors to be considered in attempting to answer are: (*a*) the specific question of greatest interest to the investigator and (*b*) what is known generally about the research area in question. Even a very experienced researcher can go astray in the choice of control groups when he or she makes a major shift of research areas. Only experience in a given research area is likely to protect the investigator from overlooking an important control group.

THE SOLOMON DESIGN: ANOTHER PARADIGM CASE

We can illustrate the complexity of the problem very well by considering a four-group research design developed by Richard L. Solomon (1949), which he and Michael Lessac (1968; Lessac & Solomon, 1969) subsequently applied in a study of the effects of isolating animals on their later adaptive behavior. While it is not a common design, it is an elegant example of the fundamental logic of the choice of adequate control groups.

Previous research had led to the development of what is called the "critical period hypothesis" (for discussion, see Columbo, 1982). This hypothesis states that there are optimum periods in the life of a baby animal during which it learns to make adaptive responses to its environment. Withholding various kinds of stimulation early in the organism's development would, it was theorized, impede the learning of sensory and motor associations important to adult behavior.

However, Solomon and Lessac questioned this hypothesis because it ignores two rival hypotheses. One rival hypothesis is that the early deprivation *destroys* an already formed behavioral organization, not one that has yet to form. The second rival hypothesis is that the early deprivation does not destroy the potential for behavior, but instead *creates* unusual patterns of responding that simply interfere with the later behaviors. To rule out these two alternative or rival hypotheses, the scientist would have to pretest the animal before it was subjected to a state of isolation. In this way, it could be established whether the animal was able to perform normally before it underwent isolation. Here is where the rub comes in! This means that the animal has had pretesting *and* isolation, not just pure isolation. The question becomes how to pretest the animal, while at the same time to control for the effects of this required pretesting.

Put another way, by pretesting the animal we can then establish whether any effects of the isolation were merely a passive arrest of learning processes or an active impediment to existing perceptual-motor patterns. Unfortunately, the pretesting as such might serve to enrich the experience of the supposedly deprived animals. It is necessary, therefore, to devise a means of determining the possible effect of the pretesting on reactions to the treatment (the isolation). This is why the four-group design was developed, and Table 5.1 shows one way of looking at it.

The Solomon design calls for subjects to be assigned to one of four groups on a purely *random* (chance) basis. Group I is pretested on whatever dependent variables are theoretically relevant, then subjected to a state of isolation, and finally retested on the dependent variables. Group II is not pretested, but undergoes the same isolation treatment and is given the same posttests as in group I. Group III is pretested and posttested, but is treated normally instead of being subjected to a period of isolation. Group IV only gets the posttests.

What can this four-group design tell us? First, by averaging the pretest performances of groups I and III we can estimate what the initial performances *would have been* in groups II and IV if they had been pretested. We assume that these pretest scores will be identical or very similar because the subjects were assigned at random. *Random assignment* tends to maximize the probability that the groups are comparable by giving each subject an equal chance of being assigned to any particular group.

Second, we can now examine the posttest performance in group II without having contaminated it by the pretesting procedures. A comparison of the estimated pretest score in group II with its actual posttest score would enable us to decide whether the isolation produced a deterioration in performance, an improvement in performance, or no effect at all. This result could then be compared with the result obtained in group IV.

Third, by comparing the differences in posttest scores between groups I and III with those found between groups II and IV—that is, $(I - III) - (II - IV)$—we can calculate the effects of the pretesting on the responses to the treatment. These effects will show whether pretesting served to increase or decrease the effect of isolation relative to the control condition.

TABLE 5.1
DIAGRAM OF THE SOLOMON FOUR-GROUP DESIGN AS USED IN A STUDY BY LESSAC AND SOLOMON (1969)

	Treatment conditions	
Procedure	Isolation	No isolation
Pretesting	I	III
No pretesting	II	IV

Solomon and Lessac used this design when they studied the critical period hypothesis with beagle pups as the subjects (Lessac & Solomon, 1969). Those pups assigned at random to groups III and IV were reared normally in the same way they would have been raised in a kennel, and those assigned at random to groups I and II were raised in isolation in 18 x 24 x 30-inch aluminum cages through which light entered by a 2½-inch space between the bottom tray and the door. All the pups were fed and medicated at the same times, and the dependent variables included testing each pup's response to pain, how it responded to its physical environment, and various tests of learning. The results of this study after one year showed that behavioral development was not merely retarded by isolation but in fact distorted.

EXPECTANCY CONTROLS: ANOTHER FOUR-GROUP DESIGN

Other specialized control group designs have been developed for a number of different purposes. For example, there is a good deal of evidence to suggest that in behavioral research the expectancy or hypothesis of the investigator can sometimes function as a self-fulfilling prophecy. That is, experimenters may sometimes communicate to their subjects how they expect the subjects to respond, and this communication can be quite subtle and unintentional (Rosenthal, 1966, 1976). A number of strategies have been developed to isolate or minimize these effects of the experimenter's expectancies.

A specialized control group design for this purpose requires that a given experiment be repeated by several experimenters, some of whom expect to find a difference between the experimental and control groups and some of whom do not. If both groups of experimenters obtain the same difference between the experimental and control groups, we can be fairly sure that the differences obtained are "real" and not due to the expectancies of the experimenters. However, if the experimenters who expect to find a difference find one, and those who do not expect to find a difference do not, we may conclude that the differences found between groups are due as much to the effects of the experimenters' expectancies as to any intrinsic difference between the experimental and control groups. When *expectancy control groups* have been employed in this way, they have shown the extent to which experimental results may be due to the effects of the experimenters' expectancies.

An example of the use of expectancy controls is shown in

Table 5.2, which also provides another example of a four-group experimental design. This experiment was performed by Cooper, Eisenberg, Robert, and Dohrenwend (1967) for the purpose of comparing the effects of experimenters' expectancies with the effects of effortful preparation for an exam on the degree of belief that the exam would actually take place. Each of 10 experimenters contacted 10 subjects; half of the subjects were required to memorize a list of 16 symbols and definitions that were claimed to be essential to the taking of an exam that had a 50-50 chance of being given, while the remaining subjects (the "low effort" group) were asked only to look over the list of symbols. Half of the experimenters were led to expect that "high effort" subjects would be more certain of actually having to take the exam, while half of the experimenters were led to expect that "low effort" subjects would be more certain of actually having to take the exam.

Table 5.2 gives the subjects' ratings of their degree of certainty of having to take the test. We see that there was a very slight tendency for subjects who had exerted greater effort to believe more strongly that they would be taking the test. We also see that experimenters expecting to obtain responses of greater certainty obtained such responses to a much greater degree than did experimenters expecting responses of lesser certainty. In this case, we might conclude that the important difference was due to the effects of the experimenters' expectancies. We would not have known this had we not used expectancy control groups.

SUMMARY

The concept of control has a number of different meanings in behavioral science, including (*a*) holding variables constant, (*b*) calibrating apparatus, (*c*) shaping behavior, and (*d*) using com-

TABLE 5.2
EXAMPLE OF THE USE OF EXPECTANCY CONTROLS

Manipulation of effort level	Expectancy controls		Row means
	High	Low	
High effort	+.64	−.40	+.12
Low effort	+.56	−.52	+.02
Column means	+.60	−.46	+.07 = Grand mean

parison groups or conditions. The fourth meaning is most central to experimental design, and we examined the logic of the use of experimental and control groups. The Solomon design was a case in point to illustrate the fundamental reasoning in choosing particular control groups to address rival hypotheses. Another specialized design used expectancy controls.

KEY TERMS

behavior control
constancy of conditions
control series
control group (versus experimental)
expectancy control groups
joint method of agreement and difference ("joint method")
method of agreement
method of difference
necessary versus sufficient condition
placebo-control group
random assignment
Solomon design
treatment condition

CHAPTER 6

REPLICATIONS AND THEIR RELATIVE UTILITY

In the behavioral sciences (as in science generally), it is not always possible to *replicate* (repeat and authenticate) every observed fact at will. Many of the empirical principles of behavior are influenced to some extent by circumstances that do not occur with any degree of predictable regularity. In this chapter, we discuss the nature of replications and their relative utility in the light of this and other practical considerations.

TACIT KNOWLEDGE

The important role of replication is well-established in science generally, even apart from its particular role in behavioral science. The undetected equipment failure, the rare and possibly random human errors of procedure, observation, recording, computation or report are well enough known to make scientists wary of the unreplicated experiment. But while replicability is universally accepted as one of the most important criteria of genuine scientific knowledge, even in natural science it is not always possible to repeat and authenticate every laboratory event at will.

Michael Polanyi (1966) introduced the concept of *tacit knowledge*, which refers to our awareness of things that we cannot easily communicate verbally—the basis of hunches and intuitions. Tacit knowledge is something we learn from direct experience and training. I know how to ride a bicycle, but I know from experience more about the skill involved than I can tell. When a novice takes a spill, he or she may conclude that no one can ride a bicycle if the skill has not been demonstrated.

Polanyi's idea helps us to understand why there are sometimes difficulties encountered when replication is attempted without the benefit of direct experience. An interesting example occurred in the 1970s, when British scientists were trying to replicate a certain form of laser experiment. The laser was invented in the 1960s, but details were not made public for several years. This laser experiment turned out to be very difficult to replicate without the benefit of previous work at the source of the original laser. It was like learning to ride a bicycle, since it called for tacit knowledge acquired through experience (Collins, 1978).

Scientists who fail to replicate an experiment, whether in behavioral or natural science, may conclude that the claimed effect is not replicable. It is also possible that the scientists who failed to replicate did not carry out the experiment "properly" because they did not have the benefit of tacit knowledge. Tacit knowledge pertaining to rat handling, for instance, is different in experimental psychology and pharmaceutical science. Experiments in these different fields require different things to be measured or held constant, all of which involves tacit knowledge (Collins, 1978).

UTILITY OF REPLICATION

Clearly the *same* experiment can never be repeated by a different worker. Indeed the *same* experiment can never be repeated by even the same experimenter (Brogden, 1951). At the very least, the subjects and the experimenters themselves are different and the experimental situation may be influenced by circumstances related to the historical period. Take, for example, the relationship between biological gender and persuasibility. Experimental studies in psychology before 1970 repeatedly found that women were more persuasible subjects then men. But studies done after 1970 showed few if any significant gender differences in persuasibility (Eagly, 1978). This suggests, as Kenneth Gergen (1973) and others have argued, that the historical period during which some experiments are conducted can serve as a powerful independent variable.

While it is not possible to have *exact* replications, it is still possible to have *relative* replications. We can rank order experiments on how close they are to each other in terms of subjects, experimenters, tasks, situations, etc. We can usually agree that *this* experiment, more than *that* experiment, is like a given paradigm study. When scientists speak of replication, they are therefore referring to a *relatively* exact repetition of an experiment.

UTILITY OF REPLICATION: WHEN, HOW, AND BY WHOM?

Some replications are more crucial than others, and three factors affecting the value or *utility* of any particular replication are: (*a*) *when* the replication is conducted, (*b*) *how* the replication is conducted, and (*c*) *by whom* the replication is conducted.

The first factor—*when* the replication is conducted—is important not only because of the possible effect of historical period, as seen in the example above, but because replicated studies conducted early in the history of a particular research question are usually more useful than replications conducted later. The first replication doubles our information about the research issue; the fifth replication adds 20 percent to our information level; and the fiftieth replication adds only two percent to our information level. Once the number of replications grows to be substantial, our need for further replication is likely to be due not to a real need for further replication, but to a real need for the more adequate evaluation and summary of the replications already available or to see how the relationship is affected by a particular historical context.

How the replication is conducted is the second important factor. It has already been noted that replications are possible only in a relative sense. If we choose our replications to be as similar as possible to the study being replicated, we may be more true to the original idea of replication but we also pay a price. That price is *external validity*, which refers to the generalizability of a causal relationship. If we conduct a series of replications as exactly like the original as we can, and if their results are consistent with the results of the original study, we have succeeded in "replicating" but not in extending the generalizability of the underlying relationship investigated in the original study. The more imprecise the replications, the greater the benefit to the external validity of the tested relationship if the results support the relationship. If the results do not support the original finding, however, we cannot tell whether that lack of support stems from the instability of the original result or from the imprecision of the replications.

The third factor—*by whom* the replicated experiment is conducted—is important because of the problem of *correlated replicators,* which we turn to next. So far in our discussion we have assumed that the replications are independent of one another. But what does "independence" mean? The usual minimum requirement for independence is that the subjects of the replications be different persons. But what about the independence of the replicators? Are a series of ten replications conducted by a single investigator as independent of one another as a series of ten replications each of which is conducted by a different investigator?

CORRELATED REPLICATORS

Scientists who have devoted their life to the study of vision, or of psychological factors in somatic disorders, are less likely to carry out a study of verbal conditioning than are scientists whose interests have always been in the area of verbal learning or interpersonal influence processes. To the extent that (*a*) experimenters with different research interests are different kinds of people and (*b*) it has been shown that different experimenters are likely to obtain different data from their subjects, we are forced to the conclusion that within any area of behavioral research the experimenters come precorrelated by virtue of their common interests and any associated characteristics. Immediately, then, there is a limit placed on the degree of independence we may expect from workers or replications in a common field. But for different areas of research interest the degree of correlation or of similarity among its workers may be quite different. Certainly we all know of workers in a common area who obtain data quite different from that obtained by colleagues. The actual degree of correlation, then, may not be very high. It may, in fact, even be negative, as with investigators who share interests in common but hold opposite expectancies about the results of any given experiment.

Contemporary research is often conducted by a team of researchers. Sometimes these teams consist entirely of colleagues. Often they are comprised of one or more faculty members and one or more students at various stages of progress toward the Ph.D. Experimenters within a single research group may reasonably be assumed to be even more highly intercorrelated than any group of workers in the same area of interest who are not within the same research group. And perhaps students in a research group are more likely to be more correlated with their major professor than would another faculty member of the research group.

There are two reasons for this likelihood. The first reason is a *selection* factor. Students may choose to work in a given area with a given investigator because of their perceived and/or actual similarity of interest and associated characteristics. Colleagues are less likely to select a university, area of interest, and specific project because of a faculty member at that university.

The second reason students may be more correlated with their professor than another professor might be is a *training* factor. Students may have had a large proportion of their research experience under the direction of a single professor. Other professors, though collaborating with their colleagues, have most often been trained in research elsewhere by other persons. While there may be exceptions, even frequent ones, it seems reasonable, on the whole, to assume that student researchers are more correlated with their advisor than another professor might be.

The correlation of replicators that we have been discussing refers directly to a correlation of *attributes* and indirectly to a correlation of *data* these investigators will obtain from their subjects. The issue of correlated experimenters or observers is by no means a new one. More than 80 years ago, Karl Pearson spoke of ". . . the high correlation of judgments . . . (suggesting) . . . an influence of the immediate atmosphere, which may work upon two observers for a time in the same manner" (1902, p. 261). Pearson believed the problem of correlated observers to be as critical for the physical sciences as for the behavioral sciences.

There is a simple principle that evolves from these considerations. It is that replications yielding consistent results are maximally informative and maximally convincing if they are maximally separated from the first experiment and from each other along such dimensions as time, physical distance, personal attributes of the experimenters, experimenters' expectancies, and experimenters' degree of personal contact with one another.

STRONG INFERENCE AND ITS LOGICAL LIMITATIONS

An idealized, optimistic approach to hypothesis testing has been described by the biophysicist J. R. Platt (1964) as the *strong inference method*. It is a little like a squirrel climbing a tree, in that at each fork the squirrel chooses to go to the right branch or to the left, until the top of the tree is reached. For the scientist the first step in strong inference is to devise alternative predictions to represent rival causal hypotheses. This is done on the basis of theory, prior observation, and the nature of the facts. The second step is to design a research study with alternative possible outcomes, each of which will (as nearly as possible) exclude one or more of the hypotheses. The third step is to carry out the research so as to get as clean a result as possible. Ideally speaking, this strong inference method is then repeated, making and testing new rival hypotheses to refine the possibilities that remain.

This approach has certain virtues, but it also has certain liabilities and shortcomings, given the probabilistic nature of our empirical principles in behavioral science. There is a possibility, for example, that when strongly divergent points of view are advocated by astute observers, *both* viewpoints may be correct in the long run. The view that was ruled out by strong inference might only be "incorrect" under the given set of circumstances in which it was immediately tested.

To give an illustration, there has been considerable research by social psychologists on the nature of the "clustering" process by which the mind consolidates related ideas and perceptions into distinct categories and stereotypes. Some researchers have argued, and indeed shown, that this clustering process involves an averaging principle; others have reported that it involves an adding principle. In fact, it is true that *both* principles are correct, but they probably apply in slightly different circumstances (Rosnow & Arms, 1968; Rosnow, Wainer, & Arms, 1970). Suppose that two persons, A and B, each have an income of $100 a day and that a third person, C, has an income of $40 a day. The total income of a group consisting of A, B, and C ($240) is higher than the total income of a group consisting only of A and B ($200), but the average income of A and B ($100) is higher than the average income of A, B, and C ($80). Were we to ask people which of these two "groups" enjoys a higher economic status, we would find that most people would answer that the group with the higher *average* income is better off financially (the averaging principle). On the other hand, if we said that these were two "families," we would find that most people would answer that the family with the higher *total* income is better off financially (the adding principle).

The point is that people do a little of both, adding and averaging. Thus, even in the case of strongly opposing principles, we might be misled if we ruled out either principle simply on the basis of a single strong inference study. The decision process will require a careful consideration of a wide range of replications done under a variety of different circumstances in order to draw appropriate boundaries around the opposing principles.

SUMMARY

Replications, while they play an important role in science, are sometimes difficult to perform when tacit knowledge is lacking or when circumstances affecting the causal relationship have changed. Further, not all replications are equally useful; it is important to consider when, how, and by whom they are done. The problem of correlated replicators, in particular, can jeopardize the external validity of the causal relationship. Strong inference is a systematic way of approaching replication by pitting rival hypotheses against one another, but it is plausible in behavioral science that even apparently contradictory hypotheses are correct (an idea to which we return in Chapter 15).

KEY TERMS

correlated replicators
external validity
selection factor (and correlated replicators)
strong inference
tacit knowledge
training factor (and correlated replicators)
utility of replication

THREE

DATA COLLECTION

CHAPTER 7

VALIDITY, RELIABILITY, AND PRECISION

In the next three chapters, we discuss some of the principles of data collection in behavioral research, beginning in this chapter with an overview of criteria for assessing the meaningfulness and accuracy of scientific observations. Three criteria that provide the underpinnings of all scientific data are their validity, reliability, and precision. Very generally speaking, *validity* refers to the degree to which scientists measure or observe what they purport to measure or observe. *Reliability* refers to the degree to which their measurements or observations are consistent. And *precision* refers to the sharpness or exactness of measurements or observations. Precision and reliability especially, but validity as well, are closely related logically and statistically, and we shall see how behavioral scientists employ these criteria in test construction and evaluation as an illustrative case.

USES OF VALIDITY IN EXPERIMENTAL RESEARCH

There are many different uses of the term "validity" in behavioral science. Validity is sometimes meant to pertain to the assessment of research conclusions or research designs and other times to the evaluation of tests or other measurements. Some typical usages would include: statistical conclusion validity, internal validity, construct validity, external validity, predictive validity, concurrent validity, and postdictive validity.

In Chapter 2, we discussed Mill's principles for unraveling causes and effects; one requirement was to show that X is at least a potential contributory condition of Y (that is to say, X and Y *covary*). *Statistical conclusion validity* is the term for this requirement. It considers the specific question as to whether the presumed independent variable, X, and the presumed dependent variable, Y, are related. If they are *not* related (that is, if X and Y do not covary), then one variable cannot have been a cause of the other.

Once we see that two variables covary, we may then want to ask whether they are causally related. *Internal validity* refers to the degree of validity of statements made about whether X causes Y. We say that a hypothetical relationship has "high internal validity" when we can rule out plausible rival hypotheses. Suppose a male and a female student decided to conduct, as a team, an experiment into the effects of stress on verbal learning. To divide the work fairly, the male experimenter might administer one treatment and the female experimenter might give the other. This design, unfortunately, has low internal validity, because it is impossible to determine whether the relationship between X (stress) and Y (verbal learning) is causal. That is, Y might have been due not to stress but to the sex of the experimenter. This problem of a plausible rival hypothesis could have been avoided by having each experimenter test half the subjects of the experimental condition and half the subjects of the control condition.

Suppose, however, that we have relatively high statistical conclusion validity and internal validity. We can say with some confidence (a) that there is a relationship between two variables and (b) that it is a plausibly causal relationship. The next question to ask is, given the plausibly causal relationship between X and Y, what are the cause and effect constructs involved in the relationships. This leads us to what is called *construct validity*, which is concerned with the psychological qualities contributing to the relationship between X and Y (Caws, 1965; Cronbach & Meehl, 1955). (It will be recalled that in Chapter 3 we discussed Crowne and Marlowe's validation of the construct of the "need for social approval.")

We might now ask: "How generalizable is the relationship between X and Y across persons, settings, and times?" *External validity* (alluded to in the preceding chapter) refers to the generalizability of a relationship beyond the circumstances under which it is observed by the scientist (Cook & Campbell, 1979).

USES OF VALIDITY IN TEST CONSTRUCTION

There are still many other uses of the term "validity" in the area known as test construction or measurement. One important type of test validity is *predictive validity*. Can the test "predict" the future? Tests of college aptitude are normally assessed for predictive validity, since the criteria of graduation and grade-point-average are events that will occur in the future. The aptitude test scores are saved until the future criterion data become available and are then correlated with them to see how well the test predicted those data.

When the criterion is in the present, we speak of *concurrent validity*. Clinical diagnostic tests are normally assessed for concurrent validity, since the criterion of the patients' true diagnostic status is in the present with respect to the tests we are trying to validate. Shorter forms of longer tests are also often evaluated with respect to their concurrent validity using the longer test as the criterion. It could reasonably be argued in such cases that it is not validity but reliability that is being assessed. Indeed, while reliability and validity are conceptually distinguishable, it is sometimes difficult to separate them in practice.

When the criterion is in the past, we speak of *postdictive validity*. Clinical tests in forensic psychiatry and psychology are normally assessed for postdictive validity since the criteria of criminal or psychopathological behavior are in the past with respect to the observations being validated. Thus, a court may want a determination of whether the accused was capable of a given unlawful act, knew at the time that it was "right" or "wrong," and was capable of controlling his or her actions. To assist the psychiatrist or psychologist in making this retrospective assessment, a psychological test of some sort may be administered. On the basis of the accused's responses, it may be decided to enter a plea of insanity when the test indicates an inability to distinguish right from wrong.

There are other types of validity to which behavioral scientists refer, although these seven give a good idea of the range of definitions and usages.

TYPES OF RELIABILITY IN TEST CONSTRUCTION

In test construction, there are three principal ways of assessing reliability: the test-retest method, the equivalent-forms method, and the method of internal consistency. Each has its own specialized usage.

The first approach, the *test-retest method*, means that data have been obtained from the same test but from results obtained at different times. The test is administered twice to the same group of people, and the objective is to determine how consistently they respond after the researcher has taken care to correct for any general effect on responding of the time interval employed or the effect of testing a second time.

Of course, when we repeatedly measure someone we do not expect to get exactly the same value each time. If we repeatedly measured a child's height, there would be small differences in the values with each measurement. The child might slouch a bit more or stand a little differently on the measuring spot or the measurer may have a slightly different angle of viewing the markings (Stanley, 1971). We would probably use the average figure, and the more highly correlated our measures, the more reliable we would conclude the measuring instrument to be.

The second approach to evaluating reliability in test construction is the *equivalent-forms method*. This approach consists of calculating the relationship, or correlation, of data from comparable forms of the same test. We might have two forms of a test of intelligence or of an attitude scale. The two forms would use different but comparable items. Both forms are administered to the same group of people, with the aim of determining whether the two forms actually measure the same (or nearly the same) thing. If the values closely converge, this means that there is high equivalent-forms reliability. The advantage in having comparable forms of an intelligence test or an attitude scale derives from the fact that familiarity with a test can often enhance performance, since subjects are apt to remember test items when tests are repeated.

The third approach to evaluating reliability in test construction is the *method of internal consistency*, in which components of the test are correlated with one another. A common example is the *split-half method*. The instrument is split in two, and both parts are administered to the same group of people. The responses to the two parts are then correlated. The objective in this case is to determine the degree to which the instrument is internally consistent.

EVALUATING ONE CRITERION WITH RESPECT TO ANOTHER

Reliability can also be evaluated in more elegant ways by employing statistical procedures other than correlations (Rosenthal & Rosnow, 1984). Whenever researchers test for reliability they must also think about validity, and vice versa. For example, in assessing the predictive, concurrent, or postdictive validity of an instrument, the researcher must try to select the most sensible and meaningful criterion that is also a reliable criterion. Grade-point-average tends to be a fairly reliable criterion in ability testing, while clinicians' judgments about complex behavior may be a less reliable criterion. One way to increase reliability in this case would be to increase the number of observations. In the same way, it is possible to increase the reliability of pooled clinical judgments by adding more clinicians to the group whose pooled judgments will serve as our criterion (Rosenthal, 1973; 1982a).

It is also important to think about the validity of the criteria that are used to assess validity. Suppose that we want to develop a short test of anxiety that will predict the scores on a longer test of anxiety. The longer test serves as our criterion, and the new short test may be relatively valid with respect to the longer test. But the longer test may be of dubious value with respect to some other criterion, for example, clinicians' judgments. Sometimes, then, criteria must be evaluated with respect to other criteria, and there are no firm rules (beyond the consensus of the researchers in an area) as to what shall constitute an ultimate criterion.

PRECISION

The third evaluation criterion, *precision*, refers to the "exactness" of scientific observations. To say that someone is "very sensitive" implies that the person possesses a high degree of susceptibility to stimulation. A person who is very sensitive to noise, for example, is someone who has a low threshold of response to the slightest sound. To say that a scientific instrument is sensitive also implies a high degree of susceptibility to stimulation. That means those who use the instrument are capable of making precise measurements, of detecting the slightest changes. Most instruments in behavioral science only approach this ideal, although some have been found capable of making relatively fine discriminations in behavior.

Besides being concerned with their instruments' degree of precision, scientists must also decide whether their measurements are more exact than is useful in a given situation, a condition called *pointless precision*. The scale in the pediatrician's office that measures a baby's weight is a more sensitive measuring instrument than the average bathroom scale. It is more precise to allow the doctor to report that the baby weighs "10 pounds and

5¾ ounces'' than to say only that the baby "tips the scale at 10 pounds.'' The precision of the latter measurement may be insufficient, but is the precision of the former measurement pointless precision? Would it be sufficient to say only that the baby weighs "10 pounds and 6 ounces"?

Loose approximation can be misleading, but the anxiety to be overly precise may reflect a lack of assurance of the scientific worth of one's endeavors (Kaplan, 1964). Thus we also speak of *false precision* when something relatively vague is reported as if the measuring instrument were sensitive to very slight variations. Suppose we asked 100 people to respond to the following attitude item:

> *Cigarette smoking is bad for your health.*
> _____ I agree strongly with this statement.
> _____ I agree moderately with this statement.
> _____ I neither agree nor disagree with this statement.
> _____ I disagree moderately with this statement.
> _____ I disagree strongly with this statement.

Let us say we numbered the responses from 1 ("agree strongly") to 5 ("disagree strongly"), then added them all up and divided by 100 to get the average response of these 100 persons. Say that the average response was in favor of the statement, and we reported that it was 1.5 or 1.55 or 1.555 or 1.5555. If we reported 1.5555 that would appear to be a more precise figure than if we said 1.5. However, the extra decimal places may add little but false precision intended to put a gloss on the data.

The precision of a particular research design can also pose a problem for scientists if it seems insensitive to the true relationships between variables. In the area of social psychology, for example, there are few reports of variables that produce *nonlinear* effects on behavior (that is, effects *not* arranged or falling on a straight line). This may be an accurate reflection of the nature of social psychological variables, but it could also be due to the imprecision of the particular research designs that were used (Converse, 1982). It is common for many researchers to explore a relationship by comparing behavior produced under a lower level of the independent variable with that produced under a higher level of the independent variable. Obviously when a study compares only two levels of a variable, it cannot detect the presence of a nonlinear relationship (assuming there is one). Only a straight line can be drawn between two points, while more than two points (or two levels) are required to reveal a nonlinear relationship. The paucity of nonlinear findings in many areas of behavioral and social science may be due, therefore, to the relative scarcity of studies that have been designed to detect them.

SUMMARY

We have looked at three criteria—precision, reliability, and validity—which are important considerations in all aspects of behavioral research. However, the most important of these three criteria is validity, for without adequate validity scientists have nothing. Internal validity is the sine qua non of experimental research. However, there are many different usages of the term validity, some pertaining to the nature of research conclusions or research designs and others to the evaluation of tests or other measurements specifically.

KEY TERMS

concurrent validity
construct validity
equivalent-forms method
external validity
false precision
internal consistency method (e.g., split-half method)
internal validity
nonlinear relationship
pointless precision
postdictive validity
predictive validity
statistical conclusion validity
test-retest method

CHAPTER 8

MEASURING HUMAN RESPONSE

Validity, reliability, and precision are criteria that help researchers to assess the utility of their measuring instruments. But these are not the only considerations that researchers must weigh, for they must also think about the circumstances in which the measurements are to be made. Sometimes it is best to disguise one's measuring instrument; other times it may be advisable to use a particular directive or nondirective strategy for asking questions. In this chapter, we look at four general classes of measuring instruments, as represented by the four cells in Figure 8.1.

STRUCTURED-UNDISGUISED MEASURES: RATING SCALES

Rating scales, which call for respondents to give numerical values to judgments or assessments, are typical of this first category of measurements. When subjects rate themselves, this is called a *self-report measure,* for example:

> Rate how *happy* you feel at this moment:
> ____ Extremely happy
> ____ Moderately happy
> ____ Neither happy nor unhappy
> ____ Moderately unhappy
> ____ Extremely unhappy

Disguised Format?

	No	Yes
Yes	I. Structured and transparent	II. Structured and indirectly disguised
No	III. Open-ended and transparent	IV. Open-ended and indirectly or unobtrusively disguised

Structured Format?

FIGURE 8.1
Four general classes of behavioral measures. By a
structured format (cells I and II) it is meant that an
instrument provides for clearcut response options. The
opposite of this is an unstructured or *open-ended format*
(cells III and IV), where respondents answer in their own
words. There are two kinds of "disguised measures." One
category refers to what are *indirectly disguised*
instruments (cells II and IV), which are characterized by
the fact that the subject is aware of being measured (or
observed) but not of the consequences of responding in
one way or another. The alternative category refers to
unobtrusive measures (cell IV), characterized by the fact
that the subject is unaware of being observed for scientific
purposes.

Rating scales are also used by researchers to give numerical
values to the behavior that *they* observe; for example, rating how
much a child tries to do well in class:

_____ Tries very, very hard
_____ Tries somewhat more than the average student
_____ Tries about like the average student
_____ Tries somewhat less than the average student
_____ Doesn't try at all

In rating scales of this form, the numerical values are implicit;
but they can also be made explicit. The following attitude item
calls for the respondent to rate his or her feelings about a particular
societal question:

Do you feel that a large-scale civil defense program would tend to incite an enemy to prematurely attack this country, or do you feel that such a program would lessen the chances of an enemy attack? (Check one)

_____ 1 It would considerably increase the chance of an enemy attack.

_____ 2 It would somewhat increase the chance of an enemy attack.

_____ 3 It would neither increase nor decrease the chance of an enemy attack.

_____ 4 It would somewhat decrease the chance of an enemy attack.

_____ 5 It would considerably decrease the chance of an enemy attack.

This type of rating scale (in which numerical values are explicit or implicit) is termed a *numerical scale*. While it is easy to construct, it has one distinct drawback when used to rate other people's behavior or personality traits, and the term *halo effect* has been coined to describe the drawback. This refers to the tendency of the rater who forms a favorable impression of someone with regard to some prominent or salient trait to then paint a rosier picture of the person on other characteristics. The halo effect can also refer to the fact that knowledge about a subject's previous outstanding performance (positive or negative) or awareness of a trait can weight the rater's assessments for better or for worse. That is, because the rater tends to judge the person being rated in terms of a general mental attitude toward him or her, this "halo" will influence the rater's opinions about specific qualities of the individual. For example, a student who was athletic or good-looking might be rated as more popular than was really the case.

To counteract the halo effect, another type of rating scale is sometimes used. Called the *forced-choice scale*, it makes the rater choose between some equally favorable or equally unfavorable statements. The rater might be asked to describe someone as either "honest" or "intelligent," but not both. The rater is thus "forced" to say that X has more of one positive trait than another equally positive trait. In developing such scales, researchers will typically run a *pilot study* (that is, try them out beforehand) on a sample of individuals like those who finally will be employed as subjects.

STRUCTURED-DISGUISED MEASURES: PERSONALITY INVENTORIES

These include self-report measures, including a number of famous personality tests. The Marlowe-Crowne Scale (discussed in Chapter 3) would fall into this category, as long as we can assume that the purpose of the test would not be transparent to the respondents; that is, the test is "indirectly disguised."

Even if the test's purpose is not immediately apparent, this does not preclude the possibility that the respondent will lie or fake his or her responses on a personality test based on what he or she *thinks* is socially desirable. As a result, many personality tests have been routinely correlated with the Marlowe-Crowne Scale, in order to detect the potential for faking.

Personality researchers have also developed keys for scoring standardized questionnaires and "lie scales" that are used to detect actual faking by the respondent (Ruch, 1942). For example, one strategy for developing a "fake key" might be to compare the responses of subjects who were instructed to fake with those of subjects who were instructed not to fake. The differences in responding between these two groups could then be used to construct a scoring key to identify subjects in future testings who were faking. Forced-choice measurements are also seen as a way of coping with actual faking, by "forcing" the respondent to accept some statements that are clearly unfavorable or to reject some statements that are clearly favorable. This procedure is thought to suppress certain defensive tendencies on the part of the respondent.

A famous personality test with its own "lie scale" is the *Minnesota Multiphasic Personality Inventory* (also called the MMPI). Structured measures such as the MMPI are paper-and-pencil tests, which are particularly useful when many subjects must be measured at once. The MMPI, which is designed to measure the respondent's personality traits, contains 550 statements like the following:

I often cross the street to avoid meeting people.
I have a great deal of stomach trouble.
I believe I am no more nervous than most others.

The subject responds to each statement by indicating whether or not it applies to him or her. An individual *profile* is then constructed, which shows the subject's relative positions on subscales of the test corresponding to personality characteristics.

UNSTRUCTURED-UNDISGUISED MEASURES: OPEN-ENDED INTERVIEWS AND QUESTIONNAIRES

These are measurements that are straightforward and also allow the respondents freedom to express themselves spontaneously. They often appear as open-ended questions in *interviews* and *questionnaires*, which are useful instruments for gathering data in a natural setting when researchers feel that persons have the language and experience to describe their own behavior. The essential difference between interviews and questionnaires, of course, is that the interviewer asks the questions directly of the subject, while in a questionnaire the subject reads the questions. An example of an open-ended question would be:

> Tell me, in your own words, what kinds of programs you like and don't like on television.

The interviewer who uses open-ended questions must be sensitive to the subtleties of what is said in order to keep asking the right questions and to keep the interview on the topic. An interesting example of this approach in behavioral science is a study done by Perry London (1970) and his colleagues. The purpose of this interview study, which was done in the 1960s, was to find out if there were character traits associated with the extremely heroic acts of Christians who risked their lives trying to save Jews in Nazi-occupied Europe during World War II.

London's strategy was to seek out both the rescuers and those who had been rescued and to do tape-recorded interviews with each person he found. Open-ended questions allowed the researchers to interview several different subject samples in the United States and Israel. The interviewer began in each case by asking the subject to describe, in his own words, incidents relevant to his wartime experiences. The interviewer then inquired about the background events that had led up to those incidents. He parenthentically asked about personal details, attitudes, and seemingly incidental variables needed to fill in the information the researchers were seeking about character traits. The interviewer worked with a checklist of content areas and questions, all of which had to be covered before the interview was completed, but the sequence of questions was left to the interviewer.

Thus, from the respondent's point of view, much of the personal information communicated was spontaneous and the interview process was friendly and informal. From the interviewer's point of view, he was able to probe sensitive areas obliquely and tactfully, yet without being secretive or deceptive and without sacrificing any questions. The results of this study suggested three propositions about character traits that seemed to be related to heroic behavior: a spirit of adventurousness, a strong sense of identification with a parental model of moral conduct, and a feeling of being a socially marginal individual.

UNSTRUCTURED-DISGUISED MEASURES: PROJECTIVE TESTS AND UNOBTRUSIVE MEASURES

This fourth category includes both hidden (unobtrusive) and indirectly disguised measurements. Personality tests such as the Rorschach Ink Blot Test and the Thematic Apperception Test are examples of indirectly disguised measures that are also unstructured in that they permit flexibility or freedom of responding.

The Rorschach is one of the oldest of projective personality measures. It was developed by the Swiss psychiatrist Hermann Rorschach in 1921. A year before his death at the age of 37, Rorschach published a thin volume, *Psychodiagnostics*, in which he reported his findings after experimenting with thousands of different blots. The test consists of 10 blots reproduced on 10 different pieces of cardboard so that they can be presented individually one after the other in a standard sequence. The respondent looks at each card for as long as he or she likes and informs the tester of whatever was perceived in the blot. The tester keeps a verbatim record of everything the subject says, noting any peculiarities of expression or unusual body movement as well. The theory behind the test is that the respondent will "project" some unconscious aspects of his or her life experience and emotions onto these ambiguous figures when responding with whatever comes to mind, hence, the name *projective test*.

Another famous projective personality test is the Thematic Apperception Test or TAT, developed by Henry A. Murray (1938, 1943). The TAT is composed of over 30 pictures of scenes of people engaged in various life contexts of which some subset is usually selected for administration. The respondent, who is led to believe that his (or her) imagination is being tested, is asked to make up a story explaining each picture: what is happening, what led up to the scene, and what will be the outcome. The tester gives particular attention to the themes behind the plots, which are presumed to disclose the respondent's concerns and personality characteristics.

For example, one TAT card shows a boy of around 10 years of age looking at a violin lying on a flat surface. A 42-year-old clerk responded as follows to this card:

> The story behind this is that this is the son of a very well-known, a very good musician and the father has probably died. The only thing the son has left is this violin which is undoubtedly a very good one and to the son, the violin is the father and the son sits there daydreaming of the time that he will understand the music and interpret it on the violin that his father had played.

The tester's interpretation of this response was that it showed preoccupation with excellence and the respondent's conviction that it is impossible to match the father's example. The clerk dreams only of things within himself; he is not motivated to act in pursuit of his own ambitions (Henry, 1956).

Unobtrusive disguised measures can encompass a wide range of possibilities. An excellent and enjoyable book on this subject is *Nonreactive Measures in the Social Sciences* (Webb, Campbell, Schwartz, Sechrest, & Grove, 1981). For example, Webb et al. mention that the degree of popularity of children's museum exhibits with glass fronts could be unobtrusively measured by comparing the number of noseprints deposited on the glass as well as by measuring the wear and tear of floor tiles in front of the cases. Degree of fear response in children could be measured by noting the shrinking diameter of a circle of seated children when they were being told a frightening ghost story. Language behavior has been unobtrusively studied by analyzing the content of messages that people composed on floor sample typewriters in department stores. Alfred Kinsey studied differences in the incidence of erotic inscriptions in graffiti in men's and women's toilets (Kinsey et al., 1953).

Various kinds of archival records are also interesting sources of unobtrusive measures; for example, checking the time interval between marriage and birth of the first child by using public marriage and birth records to get this information unobtrusively (Christensen, 1960). One researcher, on the basis of unobtrusive data he gathered from sports pages and baseball record books, found that changing a manager will usually improve a team's performance (Grusky, 1963a, 1963b). He also found that former infielders and catchers (high interaction personnel) were overrepresented among managers and that former pitchers and outfielders (low interaction personnel) were underrepresented.

Unobtrusive measures are also referred to as *nonreactive measures,* which means that they do not affect the reactions of the people being studied. *Reactive measures,* on the other hand, can alter the behavior being observed. Some researchers prefer to use disguised measurements almost routinely, particularly unobtrusive measures, on the assumption that transparent measurements may be contaminated by reactive biases.

RESPONSE SETS

Previously we referred to the halo effect, which is also one example of a *response set.* The term refers to a type of response bias in which a person's answers to questions or responses to a group of items are determined by a consistent mental set. *Yea-saying* is another example of a response set; it refers to the fact that some people like to answer "yes" to almost every statement or question, even to those items with which they may not agree!

A famous instance came to light in the 1950s with regard to a personality questionnaire called the "F Scale" (for Fascism Scale), which was developed to study the nature of the authoritarian personality. This research was begun in Germany during the 1920s, when a group of investigators at the University of Frankfurt conducted interviews with hundreds of German citizens. The results of the interviews convinced the investigators that anti-Semitic prejudices were rife in Germany and that the explosion of fascism was just a matter of time. When Hitler came to power, the researchers left Germany and emigrated to the United States. The investigation continued, with the emphasis now focused on the dissection of the fascist mentality. Working at the University of California at Berkeley, the researchers developed the F scale as a personality questionnaire that included 38 statements such as the following:

> One should avoid doing things in public which appear wrong to others, even though one knows that these things are really all right.
>
> No insult to our honor should ever go unpunished.
>
> It is essential for learning or effective work that our teachers or bosses outline in detail what is to be done and exactly how to go about it.

Such statements were thought to go together to form a syndrome of behavior that renders the person receptive to antidemocratic propaganda (Adorno, Frenkel-Brunswik, Levinson, & Sanford, 1950). This authoritarian personality was also seen as having a strong need to align himself (or herself) with authority figures and protective in-groups, a strong sense of nationalism, rigid moralism, definiteness, and a strong tendency to perceive things in absolutes, that is, as all good or all bad. Other psychological tests, including the Rorschach, were used to further describe the dynamics of the authoritarian personality.

Although this is regarded as one of the most influential studies ever done in psychology, there remained serious problems with the research. The problem that concerns us here has to do with the "unidirectional wording" of the items that comprised the F scale. If we review the sample items we see that only total disagreement with them could produce a completely nonauthoritarian score. But some amiable, obliging souls, who were not the least bit authoritarian, liked to say "yes" to every statement, apparently because they wished to gain the examiner's approval. In other words, the F Scale measured two distinct, but not readily distinguishable, character traits: authoritarianism and the agreement response set (Couch & Keniston, 1960).

To remedy this problem, what was necessary was simply to vary the wording or direction of the statements. Both positive and negative statements were eventually used in a random sequence. Thus, to obtain a completely nonauthoritarian score now required that the subject agree with some statements and disagree with others.

Response sets can also pose a problem in interview research. Studies have shown that responding is apt to be in a socially desirable direction when the subject and the interviewer are of the same race and social class (Dohrenwend, 1969; Dohrenwend, Colombotos, & Dohrenwend, 1968). The interaction then seems to take on the character of a polite social exchange. The subject has a tendency to say only what is socially desirable rather than reveal what is accurate but not desirable. One way that researchers attempt to avoid this problem is to employ interviewers who have a friendly but professional demeanor rather than interviewers who are overly solicitous (Weiss, 1970).

SUMMARY

Four general types of measuring instruments were described, based on the structure and transparency of research measures in behavioral science. Numerical scales (which are subject to a halo effect) and forced-choice scales (designed to counter halo effects) illustrate the category of structured and undisguised measurements. The Marlowe-Crowne Scale (discussed in Chapter 3) and the MMPI illustrate the category of structured and disguised (that is, indirectly disguised) measurements. Unstructured and undisguised measurements would include open-ended questionnaires and interviews. Unstructured and disguised measurements would include unobtrusive (nonreactive) procedures and indirectly disguised tests such as the Rorschach and TAT. The problem of response sets, such as the halo effect and yea-saying, requires that special precautions be taken when measuring human response.

KEY TERMS

disguised measurements (indirect and unobtrusive)
forced-choice scale
halo effect
interview
numerical scale
open-ended format (unstructured)
personality profile
pilot study
questionnaire
projective test
rating scale
reactive measure (versus nonreactive)
response set
self-report measure
structured format (versus unstructured)
yea-saying

CHAPTER 9

SELECTING RESEARCH PARTICIPANTS

We look in the dictionary when we want to determine whether or not a word has been used properly. We do this in spite of the fact that the dictionary is based on how words are in fact used—this is called the "paradox of usage." There is a paradox comparable to this one in the selection of participants for behavioral research (called the "paradox of sampling"). It derives from the fact that the appropriateness of such a selection is also validated by the method (or *sampling plan*) used to arrive at it (Kaplan, 1964). A few of the types of sampling plans that specify how participants are to be selected are discussed in this chapter, including both representative and nonrepresentative sampling.

REPRESENTATIVENESS AND PROBABILITY SAMPLING

By a *sampling plan* we mean any design or procedure that specifies how a "sample" of participants should be selected from the "population." The *sample* refers to the segment of the population for whom researchers obtain (or wish to obtain) observations, and *population* refers to the larger pool of individuals from which researchers have drawn their sample and to which they want to generalize these observations. To maximize the chances that a sample is representative of its population, a sampling plan would specify that there be no preferential selection of partici-

pants who are different from the rest of the population in any way
related to the variables under investigation.

When the sample values are in fact representative of the population, they are said to be *unbiased*. This simply means that the
sample values do not differ from the corresponding values in the
population being studied. In market research and opinion polling,
for example, the objective is to choose a sampling plan that is
"acceptably free from bias" so that the sample values can be
generalized to the population from which the respondents were
drawn.

Researchers will say that a sampling plan is acceptably free
from bias if it is a *probability sample*. In probability sampling,
every element of the population has a known (and usually equal)
probability of being selected. This probability is determined
through some process of random selection, and the most basic
random selection process is *simple random sampling*.

SIMPLE RANDOM SAMPLING

There are variations of simple random sampling that we refer to in
a moment. Since it is the simplest type of probability sampling, it
will be useful to understand something about the technique of
drawing a simple random sample before we proceed to those
more complex variations.

Simple random sampling is distinguished by the fact that the
researcher usually selects the sample elements from a table of
random digits, such as Table 9.1.

TABLE 9.1
TABLE OF RANDOM NUMBERS

10097	32533	76520	13586	34673	54876
37542	04805	64894	74296	24805	24037
08422	68953	19645	09303	23209	02560
99019	02529	09376	70715	38311	31165
12807	99970	80157	36147	64032	36653
66065	74717	34072	76850	36697	36170
31060	10805	45571	82406	35303	42614
85269	77602	02051	65692	68665	74818
63573	32135	05325	47048	90553	57548
73796	45753	03529	64778	35808	34282

Source: Rand Corporation, *A Million Random Digits with 100,000 Normal Deviates*, New
York: Free Press, 1955; reprinted by permission of Rand and the publisher.

Let us say that we wanted to select 10 men and 10 women individually at random from a population totaling 96 men and 99 women. We begin by numbering the men in the population consecutively from 01 to 96 and the women in the population consecutively from 01 to 99. We are now ready to use the random numbers table. In any use of such a table, we select the starting point blindly. Suppose we closed our eyes and put our finger blindly on the first 5-digit number on line 5 in column 1: 12807. We would read across the line two digits at a time, then across the next line, and so on, until we had chosen individually at random 10 two-digit numbers. We would then match these to the numbers we had already assigned to the men. In this case we would choose the men in the population who were numbered 12, 80, 79, 70, 15, 73, 61, 47, 64, and 03. Note that we ignored number 99 since our population was assigned numbers only ranging up to 96 for the male subjects.

We would do the same thing, beginning at another blindly chosen point, until we had chosen the 10 female subjects. In the case of a duplication we would go on to the next 2-digit number, since we do not want to test the same person twice.

There are a number of variations of simple random sampling, for example, *cluster sampling*. This consists of taking "clusters" (bunches or groups) of individuals when individual selection of subjects is too expensive. This procedure is also very useful when researchers do not have a complete directory of names of everyone in the population. In this case, the difficulty is that we cannot number the individuals in the population consecutively, which is the first step in using a table of random numbers to select names individually. Instead, following the principles of cluster sampling, the researcher would divide the population into subclasses and then sample in a way so as to ensure that each subclass is represented in proportion to its population. An illustration of this procedure is *area probability sampling,* where the clusters are chosen geographically.

SAMPLING BY CLUSTERS: AREA PROBABILITY SAMPLING

In area probability sampling, the plan consists of selecting geographical areas and then randomly subsampling for dwelling units within the selected geographical areas. Except for a minor group of transients, people can thus be identified with a place of residence, and that residence with a particular area. This procedure is usually cheaper per respondent than simple random sampling when doing a door-to-door survey.

Area probability sampling has been widely used by professional pollsters like George Gallup, Louis Harris, and others. Gallup (1976) once mentioned some of the lessons learned by him and others in 40 years of polling for political candidates, which eventually led to his and other pollsters' use of area sampling to ensure that their results were acceptably free from bias.

In the presidential election of 1936, which saw Franklin D. Roosevelt defeat Alfred Landon, a survey conducted by *The Literary Digest* registered the greatest error in the history of national public opinion polling (19 percentage points). The *Digest*, which predicted that Landon would be the victor, had chosen a large number of names from automobile lists and telephone directories for its sample. The sample turned out to be top-heavy in upper-income Republicans. The *Digest* could have used this information to correct their results, but failed to do so; instead it proudly proclaimed that the "figures had been neither weighted, adjusted, nor interpreted." The lesson learned by pollsters as a result of the debacle was that large numbers do not, in and of themselves, guarantee representativeness.

In 1940, when Roosevelt won over Wendell Willkie, pollsters first experimented with "barometer" districts and counties, a method later applied to the congressional election of 1942. They had not reckoned with voter turnout, however, which was at an all-time low because of citizens changing their place of residence to work in war factories or to enter the military. Gallup's polls correctly predicted that the Democrats would retain control of the House of Representatives, but the margin of victory turned out to be much closer than the polls predicted. The lesson learned this time was to give far more attention to the factor of voter turnout in making predictions.

In the 1948 election, Harry S Truman, by luring Democratic defectors back into the fold during the last two weeks before election day, turned the tide against his Republican opponent, Thomas F. Dewey. Public opinion polls predicted that Dewey would win, however. This time pollsters learned that their polling should be done as close to election day as possible.

After 1948, the Gallup Poll among others adopted the area sampling procedure in which election districts were randomly selected throughout the nation and then households within these districts were contacted by interviewers. Using this procedure and the lessons learned from the mistakes made in previous polls, enormous improvements have resulted. Prudent poll watchers now can expect an error of only two to three percentage points in national elections.

NONRESPONSE BIAS AND VOLUNTEER BIAS

Not everyone who is contacted by an opinion pollster will agree to participate. In fact, it is almost impossible to obtain answers from every person in a large sample no matter what sampling plan is used. For this reason, strategies have been developed for estimating "bias due to nonresponse," or simply *nonresponse bias*. Strategies have also been developed for stimulating and thus increasing participation.

For example, the follow-up or reminder using a telephone call, a registered letter, or a special delivery letter has been found to be an especially effective technique for stimulating responses to mailed questionnaires (Linsky, 1975). Another technique that has proven effective in mail surveys is to contact the potential respondents before they receive the questionnaire in order to encourage their later participation. Researchers also prefer to send out the questionnaire using a "high-powered mailing" such as special delivery or airmail, and using hand-stamped rather than postage-permit return envelopes.

A variation on nonresponse bias, called *volunteer bias*, is another problem for consideration. The problem in experimental research is that many subjects are volunteers, who may be different from nonrespondents or nonvolunteers in ways that are related to the nature of the investigation. For instance, brighter individuals might be more likely to volunteer for an experiment in learning, and gregarious individuals might choose an experiment in small group interactions. The extent to which these subjects are different from those persons who do not respond may have serious effects on estimates of many population values.

Fortunately, a great deal has been learned in recent years about the characteristics of the typical volunteer subject and the types of situations that are conducive to volunteering, so that it is possible to deal with volunteer bias almost as effectively as pollsters deal with the problem of nonrespondent bias. To illustrate, suppose an investigator were interested in the effects of some unusual treatment on the dependent variable of psychological adjustment or pathology. Since there is evidence to suggest that volunteer subjects, especially in clinical investigations, tend to be more maladjusted than nonvolunteers, it logically follows that any unusual manipulation designed to increase psychological adjustment might be judged as more effective than it would actually be in the general population. The problem is one of "ceiling effects," in that maladjusted subjects would have more room in which to improve than would normal subjects, who start closer to the ceiling of adjustment (Rosenthal & Rosnow, 1975).

NONRANDOMIZED SELECTION IN EXPERIMENTAL AND QUASI-EXPERIMENTAL RESEARCH

Laboratory experiments are not the only studies in which *nonrandomized* selection is typical. Often researchers take whatever subjects are available (or whatever groups are available), and these subjects may also already belong to existing groups. In educational research, for example, the investigators may not have a choice as to the groups to which the participants will be assigned. This poses obvious difficulties for causal inferences, since in nonrandom selection one does not have pre-experimental equivalence of groups. The term "quasi-experimental design" is used to refer to any such nonrandom design that resembles an experiment (in that there may be treatments, outcome measures, and experimental units) but there is no random assignment to treatments to create the equivalence of groups from which treatment-caused changes are usually inferred.

One final illustration of nonrandomized selection occurs in what is often referred to as "small-N research" or "single case research" (Kazdin & Tuma, 1982). Animal conditioning studies using small samples of partially or fully inbred strains of rats, mice, rabbits, etc., would be an example. It is assumed that genetic differences are minimized or eliminated by means of the breeding schedule and that experiments using a particular strain of animals can also be more easily replicated in different laboratories. The typical approach involves monitoring the animals' performance continuously within separate phases while specific conditioning treatments are introduced. Changes in the pattern of performance serve as the basis for drawing inferences about treatment effects.

Part of the reasoning behind small-N research is that the study of ongoing behavior in a highly controlled situation gives the experimenter an important tactical advantage. The behavior can be manipulated to serve as a *baseline* from which to measure the effects of the experimental operations (the treatments). Once such a behavioral baseline has been established, it is assumed that the researcher can generalize to other subjects because their baselines are equatable. Should there be any residual variability, however, the procedure would then be to search for previously overlooked sources of differences in order to impose comparability on the data (Sidman, 1960).

Just as the choice of an appropriate sampling plan is a basic consideration, so is the original decision to conduct the investigation using one set of procedures as opposed to another. The usual reason for using volunteer subjects, for instance, is to allow potential participants the freedom of exercising an informed decision on whether or not to participate. So far the discussion has emphasized the scientific values that are taken into consideration; in later chapters, we shall discuss the ethical values which must also be considered.

SUMMARY

Sampling plans that specify how participants are to be randomly selected are scientists' theoretical means of validating the representativeness of their subjects. In survey research, for example, there are several variations of random sampling, including area probability sampling, that are used by professional pollsters and social scientists. Not everyone who is invited to participate will respond affirmatively, however, and there are strategies for dealing with response bias and volunteer subject bias. In much behavioral research, nonrandomized selection is typical. In what are called "small-N" studies, as in animal conditioning research, the researchers start by establishing a behavioral baseline for each subject. Typically these studies use partially or fully inbred animals, on the assumption that genetic differences are minimized or eliminated by the breeding schedule.

KEY TERMS

area probability sampling
baseline
ceiling effect
cluster sampling
nonresponse bias
nonrandomized selection
population
probability sample
quasi-experimental design
sample
sampling plan
sampling units
simple random sampling
small-N research
unbiased sample
volunteer bias

DATA ANALYSIS

CHAPTER 10

DESCRIBING DATA

One aim of the analysis of data is to discover patterns or nonrandom clusters of data points by the use of statistical formulas. In the following three chapters, we discuss the rudimentary logic of several standard methods of statistical analysis used by researchers. In these chapters, we are more interested in the intuitive basis of data analysis than in the mathematical calculations (which are alluded to in these chapters but are discussed in more detail in the appendix of this book). We begin with the problem of how best to describe data, since much of the fundamental analysis of data consists of describing groups of *sampling units*; these are groups of persons or things (countries, states, cities, precincts, classrooms, wards, etc.) that are taken as our units of analysis. A number is assigned to each sampling unit on some particular variable. The task of describing the data then involves summarizing the numbers representing the sampling units on that variable.

DISPLAYING DATA

Since graphical displays of data can provide vivid summaries of research findings that allow investigators to see meaningful patterns in the data, researchers frequently look for ways of arranging their observations using graphics. For our example, let us suppose we have measured nine people on a scale of anxiety and obtained the following numbers: 5, 8, 7, 6, 4, 6, 7, 5, and 6. We might begin by ordering these numbers from lowest to highest to get a better view of their beginning and ending points and where they clump or bunch: 4, 5, 5, 6, 6, 6, 7, 7, 8. It is now possible to display them in a graphic called a *frequency distribution,* as illustrated in Figure 10.1. This figure reduces the number of categories to a curve reflecting the frequency of occurrence of different score values.

We see that the score values of this frequency distribution increase from left to right, and that the height of the curve reflects the frequency of occurrence of the scores. Note that one axis is labeled X and the other Y. When describing experimental findings, researchers usually plot the independent variable on the X-axis and the dependent variable on the Y-axis. Thus distributions of experimental research data will show the rise and fall of frequencies as our eye moves over varying values of the independent variable. Another name for the horizontal or X-axis is the *abscissa,* and another name for the vertical or Y-axis is the *ordinate.*

MEASURES OF LOCATION

One characteristic of frequency distributions that researchers almost always want to know is the location of their bulk, or the central or typical values. In this distribution, we see that the central or typical value, where the numbers bunch, is 6. Three measures commonly used to describe location are the mode, median, and mean—which in the case of a typical symmetrical distribution (such as the one shown here) will be identical values. However, the mode, median, and mean are not always identical, and which one researchers choose will depend on the situation and on their knowledge of the properties of each measure.

FIGURE 10.1
A distribution showing the frequency of occurrence of different score values.

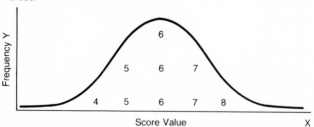

The *mode* is the score that occurs with the greatest frequency. It is the simplest to determine and also the least sensitive to extreme values. In the series of scores, 3, 4, 4, 4, 5, 5, 6, 6, 7, the modal score is 4. The series 3, 4, 4, 4, 5, 5, 6, 7, 7, 7 has two modes (at the values 4 and 7) and is called *bimodal*.

The *median*, which is relatively easy to compute, is the mid-most score in a series of ordered scores when the number of scores (N) is an odd number. When N is an even number, the median is half the distance between the two midmost numbers. Take the series 2, 3, 3, 4, 4, 5, 6, 7, 7, 8, 8—where N is an odd number ($N = 11$ scores)—and we see that the median value is 5. In the series 2, 3, 3, 4, 4, 7—where N is an even number ($N = 6$ scores)—the median value is 3.5, that is, half-way between the 3 and the 4 at the center of the set of scores.

Ties create a problem. The series 3, 4, 4, 4, 5, 6, 7 has one score below 4 and three above, four scores below 5 and two above, four scores below 4.5 and three above. In this case, a useful procedure is to view the series as perfectly ranked so that a series 1, 2, 3, 3, 3 is seen as made up of a 1, a 2, a small 3, a larger 3, and a still larger 3. The assumption is that more precise measurement procedures would have allowed us to break the ties. Thus in the series 1, 2, 3, 3, 3, we would regard 3, the ''smallest 3,'' as the median, since there are two scores below this particular 3 and two above it.

The *mean*, which is symbolized as $\bar{X}$, is the most frequently used of the three measures. It is the arithmetic average of the scores, that is, the sum of the scores divided by the number of scores. A standard formula for the ordinary mean (or *arithmetic mean*) is

$$\bar{X} = \frac{\Sigma X}{N}$$

The term Σ tells us to sum the X scores. In the series 1, 2, 3, 3, 3, the sum of the scores is 12, that is, $\Sigma X = 12$. The number of scores is 5, that is, $N = 5$. Therefore, the mean is 2.4.

When distributions are strongly asymmetrical, researchers may prefer *trimmed means* to ordinary means. This is because ordinary means are the most sensitive to extreme values. We trim by dropping a particular percentage of the scores from both ends of the distribution and computing the mean of the remaining scores. Trimming 10 percent of the scores from each end of the following series, −20, 2, 3, 6, 7, 9, 9, 10, 10, 10, would give us a trimmed mean of 7.0. The median is unaffected by trimming, so the median of these same data is eight with or without trimming.

The mode, which may be affected by trimming, is 10 before trimming but bimodal at 9 and 10 after trimming.

Medians and trimmed means protect researchers from possibly misleading interpretations based on a few extreme or very unusual scores. For example, if we listed the family income for 10 families and found nine of them with zero income and one with a $10 million income, the mean income of $1 million would be highly unrepresentative compared to the trimmed mean or median (or in this case, even the mode) of zero income. We could, however use two measures to describe the situation. If we used the mode and the mean, we would suggest that the largest number of people in this particular sample were in abject poverty, but that there was enormous wealth in the sample nonetheless.

MEASURES OF SPREAD

Besides knowing the central tendency (or typical value of a sampling unit), researchers almost always want to know about the degree to which values deviate from these measures of central tendency (that is, how spread out the scores are). Several measures of spread, dispersion, or variability are commonly used, including the range, average deviation, variance, and standard deviation.

The *range* is the distance between the highest and lowest scores. In the series 2, 3, 4, 4, 6, 7, 9, we define the *crude range* as the highest score (9) minus the lowest score (2), to give us $9 - 2 = 7$.

A refinement is often introduced that takes into account the fact that a score of 9 might, under conditions of more precise measurement, fall somewhere between 8.5 and 9.5, while a score of 2 might, under conditions of more precise measurement, fall somewhere between 1.5 and 2.5. This is called the *extended range* (or corrected range), and in this case it runs from a high of 9.5 to a low of 1.5, so that $9.5 - 1.5 = 8$. The use of the extended range adds a half unit at the top of the distribution and a half unit at the bottom of the distribution, or a total of one full unit. Thus the extended range is defined as the highest score (H) minus the lowest score (L) plus one unit, or $H - L + 1$.

For most practical purposes, researchers use either the crude or extended range. When measurement is not very precise and when the crude range is small, they obtain a more accurate picture of the actual range by using the extended range. Suppose a researcher were using a 3-point rating scale and all the judges made ratings at the midpoint value, 2 on a scale of 1 to 3. Then the crude range would be 0 (2 − 2), but the extended range would be 1 (2.5 − 1.5). The assumption is that some of the judges might have rated nearly as high as 2.5 and some nearly as low as 1.5 had those ratings been possible.

The *average deviation, $\bar{D}$,* tells the average distance from the mean of all the scores in the series. To compute $\bar{D}$ we subtract the mean of all the scores ($\bar{X}$) from each individual score (X) in turn, sum these differences disregarding the algebraic signs, and divide by the number of scores (N) in the series:

$$\bar{D} = \frac{\Sigma \mid X - \bar{X} \mid}{N}$$

Let us try an example. Given a series of scores 4, 5, 5, 6, 10, we find the mean to be 30/5 = 6. We now subtract 6 from each individual score and sum the absolute values (that is, the differences disregarding algebraic signs). This gives us 2 + 1 + 1 + 0 + 4, or $\Sigma \mid X - \bar{X} \mid$ = 8. Dividing this number by N = 5 gives an average deviation of 1.6. We can see that the average deviation uses more of the information in a series of scores than does the range (which uses only the largest and smallest scores), but we can also see that $\bar{D}$ is less convenient to compute than the range.

The most widely used of all measures of dispersion, spread, or variability is the *standard deviation,* which is the square root of another measure called the *variance.* The simple variance, symbolized as σ^2, is used as a measure of the extent to which individual values differ from each other on the average. It is statistically defined as the mean of the squared deviations of the individual scores in a set of scores from their mean, or

$$\sigma^2 = \frac{\Sigma(X - \bar{X})^2}{N}$$

The standard deviation, symbolized as σ, is simply the square root of this value, or

$$\sigma = \sqrt{\frac{\Sigma(X - \bar{X})^2}{N}}$$

To see how the mean, variance, and standard deviation would be computed on the same distribution of sampling units, let us take a set of six raw scores: 2, 4, 4, 5, 7, 8. We can set up the simple calculations required in the form of a summary table, as shown in Table 10.1. The sum of the first column provides us with the numerator of the computation formula for the arithmetic mean, and the number of scores in this column provides us with the denominator of the formula:

TABLE 10.1

SUMMARY DATA REQUIRED TO COMPUTE THE MEAN, VARIANCE, AND STANDARD DEVIATION

Raw scores	$X - \bar{X}$	$(X - \bar{X})^2$
2	−3	9
4	−1	1
4	−1	1
5	0	0
7	2	4
8	3	9
$\Sigma X = 30$		$\Sigma(X - \bar{X})^2 = 24$

$$\bar{X} = \frac{\Sigma X}{N} = \frac{30}{6} = 5$$

We now use this mean to calculate the values in the second column, which were arrived at by subtracting the mean from each raw score. Squaring each of these difference scores gives us the third column, and the sum of the values in this column provides the numerator of the formula for the simple variance:

$$\sigma^2 = \frac{\Sigma(X - \bar{X})^2}{N} = \frac{24}{6} = 4$$

Finally, the square root of the variance gives us the standard deviation:

$$\sigma = \sqrt{\sigma^2} = \sqrt{4} = 2$$

THE NORMAL DISTRIBUTION

When scores on a variety of types of sampling units in biology, psychology, and sociology are collected using a representative sampling procedure (such as that discussed in the preceding chapter), the distribution of these scores will typically form a curve that has a distinct bell-like shape. We call this curve a *normal distribution* because of the large number of different kinds of data that are assumed to be distributed in this manner. The normal distribution can be completely described from just our knowledge of the mean and standard deviation, and it is especially useful because researchers can specify what proportion of the area is to be found in any region of the curve. Figure 10.2 depicts areas in various segments of the normal distribution divided into standard deviation units.

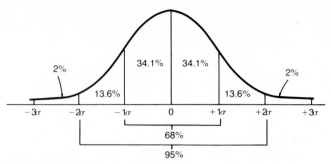

FIGURE 10.2
The normal distribution divided up into standard deviation units.

We see that about two-thirds of the scores fall between -1σ and $+1\sigma$, and about 95 percent of the scores fall between -2σ and $+2\sigma$. Over 99 percent of the scores fall between -3σ and $+3\sigma$, but the tails of the normal curve never do quite touch down. Because it is assumed that so many kinds of data are distributed normally, this bell-shaped curve and the statistics derived from it are very important for the testing of hypotheses in many research areas of behavioral science.

A normal curve such as this one, with mean set at 0 and σ set equal to 1, is specifically called a *standard normal curve*. Any score obtained on any normally distributed measure can be transformed into a score corresponding to a location on the abscissa of a standard normal curve. This is done by subtracting from the obtained score the mean obtained score and dividing this difference by the standard deviation of the original distribution. For example, assuming a mean $(\bar{X})$ of 500 and standard deviation (σ) of 100 for the SAT tests, an obtained SAT score of 625 is equivalent to a standard deviation score (or Z score) of 1.25. That is,

$$Z \text{ score} = \frac{X - \bar{X}}{\sigma} = \frac{625 - 500}{100} = 1.25$$

A positive Z score is above the mean of zero; a negative Z score is below the mean. An important use of Z scores is to permit the comparison (and the averaging) of scores from distributions of widely differing means and standard deviation. For example, by computing Z scores for height and weight, a researcher can tell whether a person is taller than he or she is heavy, relative to others in the distribution of height and weight.

Or suppose a teacher had two measures of course grades, one based on a midterm multiple-choice exam of 100 points with $\bar{X} = 70$ and $\sigma = 12$, another on a final essay exam of 10 points with $\bar{X}$

= 6 and σ = 1. It would make no sense to sum or average a person's scores on the two exams. An example is shown in Table 10.2. At the top we see the raw scores for three students—Sheila, Mimi, and Connie—who each earned a total of 76 points on two exams. If the teacher converted each raw score to a standard score (Z score), that would give the results shown in the bottom half of the table. Sheila scores at the mean both times. Mimi was slightly above average on the first test but far below average on the second. Connie was slightly below average on the first test but far above average on the second test. The sums and averages of the Z scores take these facts into account, while the sums and averages of the raw scores are quite misleading as indices of these students' course performance.

SUMMARY

Describing sampling units, based on pictorial summaries or on statistical measures of location and spread, constitutes the most fundamental quantitative analysis of research data. The mode, median, and mean are the three measures of central tendency most commonly referred to in behavioral research. When distributions are symmetrical, these values are typically identical, but when distributions are strongly asymmetrical, researchers often prefer to use more than one measure of location. The range, average deviation, variance, and standard deviation are the most commonly used measures of spread or variability. The normal distribution, which is a bell-shaped curve, can be completely described by the mean and standard deviation, which are also the basis of Z scores.

TABLE 10.2
RAW SCORES AND STANDARD DEVIATION SCORES ON TWO EXAMS

Student	Exam I	Exam II	Total	Average
Raw scores				
Sheila	70	6	76	38
Mimi	73	3	76	38
Connie	67	9	76	38
Standard deviation scores				
Sheila	0.00	0.00	0.00	0.00
Mimi	0.25	−3.00	−2.75	−1.38
Connie	−0.25	3.00	2.75	1.38

KEY TERMS

abscissa versus ordinate
average deviation
crude range (versus extended range)
frequency distribution
mean (arithmetic versus trimmed)
median
mode (bimodal distribution)
normal distribution
standard deviation
standard normal curve ($\bar{X} = 0$, $\sigma = 1$)
sampling unit
variance
Z score (standard deviation score)

CHAPTER 11

ESTABLISHING RELATIONSHIPS

Since all science requires that researchers view facts not as isolated but as related or connected in systematic and meaningful ways, one major objective is to identify these meaningful relationships. To make sense of the chaos of what may appear to be unconnected elements, researchers look for *correlations* (mutual relationships) of two or more measurements. One of a number of statistical measures of correlation is Karl Pearson's *product-moment correlation coefficient,* or the Pearson *r*. There are a great many other tests and measures of relationship that are all related to one another in various ways, but there is no more widely employed measure of the extent of linear correlation between two variables than the Pearson *r*.

ILLUSTRATION OF PEARSON *r*

The Pearson *r* quantifies the nature and extent of linear relationships being examined. Pearson *r*'s can range from -1.0 through 0 to $+1.0$. A value of 0 means that there is no linear relationship between the two variables being examined. A value of $+1.0$ means that there is a perfect positive linear relationship between them; that is, as scores on one variable increase, there are perfectly predictable *increases* in the scores on the other variable. A value of -1.0 means that there is a perfect negative linear rela-

TABLE 11.1
RAW DATA FOR FOUR SUBJECTS ON TESTS X AND Y

	Test X	Test Y	Test X	Test Y	Test X	Test Y
Subject 1	8	16	8	6	8	−4
Subject 2	6	12	6	4	6	−3
Subject 3	4	8	4	4	4	−2
Subject 4	2	4	2	6	2	−1
		$r = +1.0$		$r = .0$		$r = -1.0$

tionship between the variables; that is, as scores on one variable increase, there are perfectly predictable *decreases* in the scores on the other variable.

These three possibilities ($r = +1.0$; $r = .0$; $r = -1.0$) are illustrated in Table 11.1 for a sample of four subjects, each of whom has been measured on two personality tests that are arbitrarily labeled X and Y. A way of representing these relationships pictorially is to use a *scatterplot*, which is simply a graph that plots each mutual observation of X and Y as a point. Scatterplots, as illustrated by the ones shown in Figure 11.1, are useful means of visually determining whether X and Y are linearly related in a positive or a negative way. This figure shows that two variables can be perfectly correlated (in the sense of $r = +1.0$ or -1.0) even though the scores on X and Y never agree.

FIGURE 11.1
Scatterplots for the data shown in Table 11.1, which illustrate r's of +1.0, .0, and −1.0.

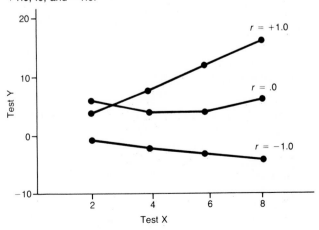

INTERPRETING *r* AS EFFECT SIZE

A useful characteristic of *r* is that when squared it tells us the amount of variation in one variable estimable from the other. This is specifically referred to as the *proportion of variance accounted for,* that is:

$$r^2 = \text{proportion of variance accounted for}$$

Put another way, r^2 is the amount of variation shared by X and Y. For example, a positive or negative Pearson *r* of 1.0 (in which case r^2 also equals 1.0) means that the variation among the Y scores is perfectly attributable to the variation in the X scores, and vice versa.

In Chapter 4, we introduced the concept of *effect size*, which refers to the degree to which the relationship studied differs from zero. Effects are customarily referred to as "small," "medium," or "large" depending upon the proportion of variance accounted for. In the case of *r*—following the convention proposed by Cohen (1969, 1977)—it is increasingly common in behavioral science to use these labels as defined in Table 11.2.

In Chapter 4, we also noted an example in which one investigator (Smith) reported a significant relationship between *X* and *Y*, only to have another investigator (Jones) publish a rebuttal claiming that there is no such relationship. In that example, Smith reported a relationship with an alpha less than 1 in 20, but Jones (who used half as many subjects as Smith) published a relationship with an alpha greater than 3 in 10. The conventional symbol for these probabilities is *p*, so that Smith would report $p < .05$ (read as "probability less than 5 in 100") and Smith would report

TABLE 11.2
A COMMON INTERPRETATION OF EFFECT SIZE AS "SMALL," "MEDIUM," OR "LARGE"

Effect size	r^*	r^2
Small	.1	.01
Medium	.3	.09
Large	.5	.25

*It makes no difference whether *r* is positive or negative. The *percentage* of variation accounted for by each *r* in this column would be obtained by multiplying the values shown in the column of r^2's by 100, since r^2 represents the *proportion* of variation accounted for.

$p > .3$ (read as "probability greater than 3 in 10"). We also said that a closer look at Jones's study showed not only that his results were in the same direction as Smith's, but that the effect size was exactly the same in both studies.

In other words, both sets of findings accounted for the same proportion of variance (r^2) based on the same correlation (r). This occurred even though the levels of significance (p) were different, due to the fact that Jones's sample size (N) was so much smaller than Smith's. We can now restate the results of these two studies as follows, where we see that Smith's results are more significant than Jones's, but the studies are in perfect agreement on their estimated effect size as defined by r:

Smith's study: $r^2 = .06, r = +.24, p < .05, N = 40$
Jones's study: $r^2 = .06, r = +.24, p > .3, N = 20$

Clearly Jones was wrong in insisting that he had failed to replicate Smith's results.

INTERPRETING r WITH REFERENCE TO BESD

We have seen how it is better to evaluate the results of a study by considering the effect size as well as the significance level. Although we have used the labels of "small," "medium," and "large" to denote particular sizes of r, the practical meaning of an effect size still may not be intuitively clear. To help understand it better, we now refer to what is known as the "binomial effect-size display" or BESD (Rosenthal & Rubin, 1979, 1982). BESD takes its name from the fact that it displays the change in success rate on some dependent variable into dichotomous (or binomial) outcomes, such as success versus failure, improved versus not improved, or survived versus died. The specific question addressed by BESD is the magnitude of the effect of some independent variable (X) on the dependent variable (Y), where Y is defined as the *success rate* (that is, the survival rate, cure rate, improvement rate, selection rate, etc.).

For our example we will use improvement rate as the success rate dependent variable, although we want to emphasize that the interpretation of BESD is not affected by the choice of dependent variable. Table 11.3 corresponds to an r of .32, which means $r^2 = .10$. For convenience and consistency the row and column totals are usually set to 100, but the original data yielding the r that a researcher may want to display do not require equal or fixed totals.

TABLE 11.3
BESD CORRESPONDING TO AN r OF .32

	Outcome		
	Improved	**Not improved**	**Σ**
Experimental group	66	34	100
Control group	34	66	100
Σ	100	100	200

The table tells us that to have an r as large as .32 (previously referred to as a "medium effect") will correspond to increasing the success rate from 34 percent to 66 percent. Suppose our independent variable were a new drug to reduce hypertension (high blood pressure). Given $N = 200$ subjects, half assigned to the experimental group and half to the placebo control group, this means that two-thirds of the subjects in the experimental group will have shown improvement as a consequence of being given the drug compared to only one-third improvement in this hypothetical case in the placebo group.

One great convenience of BESD, the name for this kind of pictorial display, is the ease with which we can convert it to r (or r^2) and the ease with which we can go from r (or r^2) to the display. Table 11.4 shows the systematic increase in success rates associated with various values of r^2 and r. For example, an r of .30, which accounts for 9 percent of the variance, is associated with an increase in the success rate from 35 to 65 percent. The last column of the table shows that the difference in success rate is identical to r. Consequently, the experimental group success rate in the BESD is computed as $.50 + r/2$, and the control group success rate is computed as $.50 - r/2$ (Rosenthal, 1982b).

CORRELATIONS IN CROSS-LAGGED DATA ANALYSIS

Correlations can be used to probe for causal relationships in research employing *cross-lagged data*. The term simply means that one variable lags temporally behind the other, and we shall look at an actual example to see how this works. In this example, the researchers were interested in the relationship between television violence and aggression (Eron, Huesmann, Lefkowitz, & Walder, 1972).

The researchers had access to data on the television viewing habits of a sample of children in the third grade and also peer

TABLE 11.4
INCREASES IN SUCCESS RATES CORRESPONDING TO VALUES OF r^2 AND r

r^2	r	Success rate increased		Difference in success rates
		From	To	
.01	.10	.45	.55	.10
.04	.20	.40	.60	.20
.09	.30	.35	.65	.30
.16	.40	.30	.70	.40
.25	.50	.25	.75	.50
.36	.60	.20	.80	.60
.49	.70	.15	.85	.70
.64	.80	.10	.90	.80
.81	.90	.05	.95	.90
1.00	1.00	.00	1.00	1.00

ratings of their aggressiveness, which they got by posing the question "Who started fights over nothing?" The actual correlation between these two variables was $+.21$, somewhere between "small" and "medium" and is associated with a difference in success rate of .21, which is not too bad. However, we do not know which of these two variables (preference for violent TV or aggressiveness) is the independent variable and which is the dependent variable. All we know is that the children who watched more violent TV were also the more aggressive. (If the relationship had been negative, that would have told us that the children who watched more violent TV were less aggressive.) In other words, there are three good rival hypotheses to consider: (*a*) aggression is the independent variable and the preference for violent TV is the dependent variable; (*b*) aggression is the dependent variable and the preference for TV violence is the independent variable; and (*c*) both are dependent variables and some other variable is their common cause.

One way to unravel the puzzle of causality is to look at the relationships between these two variables over time, by employing cross-lagged correlations. By examining the *cross-correlations* it may be possible partially to rule out one or more of the rival hypotheses and narrow the field a little. A great deal has been said about this procedure, but we shall only look at the obvious possibilities (see Kenny, 1979, for detailed discussion). Figure 11.2 shows the results obtained when these same children were tested 10 years later (in the "13th grade").

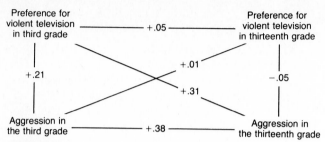

FIGURE 11.2
Correlations for two variables: (a) preferences for violent television and (b) aggression. The diagonal lines show the direction of the two cross-lagged correlations, based on research by Eron, Huesmann, Lefkowitz, and Walder (1972).

You will recall that one criterion of causality is that two variables are actually related. In this case, we can establish whether the variables are related by examining the correlations between them within the period of time when the students were in the 3rd grade ($r = +.21$) and when they were in the 13th grade ($r = -.05$). Since the first correlation is satisfactorily high, it leads us to believe that the two variables are related, at least in the 3rd grade sample. It is curious that the correlation is only minuscule in the 13th grade, but maybe by that time the aggressive children were bored with television and were pursuing other aggressive activities.

We can also examine the measures of the two variables to see whether or not they are stable (reliable) measures. This can be established by examining the top and bottom correlations ($r = +.05$ and $r = +.38$). There is not much stability at all between the measures of the children's preference for violent TV taken 10 years apart from one another, but there is some stability in the measures of aggressive behavior taken 10 years apart from one another.

The key question, however, is whether there is evidence of a causal relationship. The cross-lagged correlations give us a clue as to whether there is or is not a causal relationship between these two variables. One cross-lagged correlation ($r = +.31$) involves the relationship between preference for watching violent TV in the 3rd grade and aggression in the 13th grade. The other correlation ($r = +.01$) involves the relationship between aggression in the 3rd grade and preference for violent TV in the 13th grade. The minimal correlation between aggression in the 3rd grade and preference for violent TV in the 13th grade, especially in relation to the larger correlation between preference for violent TV in the

3rd grade and aggression in the 13th grade, seems to weaken the possibility that aggressiveness is the independent variable and the preference for violent TV is the dependent variable. That there is a much stronger correlation between preference for violent TV in the 3rd grade and aggression in the 13th grade, than between aggression in the 3rd grade and preference for violent TV in the 13th grade, seems to suggest that watching violence on television is causally implicated in the relationship between these two variables.

Nevertheless, the findings are only suggestive. We would want to look at a wide range of similar data to see whether the original cross-lagged relationships can be replicated in other samples at other periods. These particular findings, incidentally, which have in fact been replicated in other countries, have been widely quoted as evidence for the danger of watching TV violence (Eron & Huesmann, 1980).

SUMMARY

The interpretation of correlations such as the Pearson r permits researchers to view facts as related or connected in meaningful ways. The Pearson r, which can vary from -1.0 to $+1.0$, measures the extent of linear correlation between two variables. Standard interpretations of r include those based on the proportion of variance, r^2, held in common between the variables. The binomial effect-size display, or BESD, is useful for getting an intuitive grasp of what different effect sizes mean when one variable can be regarded as an independent variable. BESD interprets the effect size in terms of "improvement in success rate." In evaluating the results of a study, it is prudent to look at the effect size as well as the significance level (p value). Correlations, however, need to be interpreted within the particular context of the variables to which they apply, and in some cases they can be used to probe for causal relationships even when experimental manipulation and random assignment have not been employed.

KEY TERMS

BESD
cross-lagged data
effect size (small, medium, large)
Pearson r
proportion of variance
scatterplot
success rate (as general dependent variable)

CHAPTER 12

COMPARING EFFECTS

Besides describing data (Chapter 10) and establishing relationships (Chapter 11), another typical concern of investigators is the comparison of research groups. The fact that the employment of more than one control group is possible in arranging to make experimental observations (as in the case of the Solomon design discussed in Chapter 5) suggests that investigators must make decisions about the specific control groups as well as the experimental groups that are to be included in their research. Particularly in some of its more statistical aspects, the design of experiments and the comparison of research groups is a very specialized and highly developed field. In this chapter, we discuss three basic designs that are known generally to researchers: randomized designs, factorial designs, and repeated-measures designs. These are the research designs that are employed in the vast majority of behavioral experiments in which researchers are interested in comparing effects.

RANDOMIZED DESIGNS: TWO CONDITIONS

To review several pertinent concepts we will begin with the analogy of the college admissions officer who, when faced with a candidate for admission, must decide between two alternatives. One possibility is that the prospective student will succeed if admitted; the other is that the required work is beyond the applicant's ability and that the student will flunk out if admitted. If the admissions officer rejects the student and the student could have done well, the officer commits one type of error. If, on the other hand, the admissions officer accepts the student and the student flunks out, the officer commits another type of error.

Like the admissions officer, the behavioral researcher is also dealing with a relatively uncertain situation in testing a specific null hypothesis against a working hypothesis. The researcher will see if it is possible to reject the null hypothesis and yet be reasonably sure that, when this is done, he or she will not be wrong in doing so.

Suppose a researcher has conducted an experiment on the effect of vitamins on the academic performance of ghetto children. The research plan used is a common one, called a *simple randomized design*, in which there are two groups (an experimental group and a control group) to be compared on the dependent variable and the children are placed in their particular group at random so that no sampling bias can enter into their assignment to experimental conditions. The experimenter's working hypothesis is that vitamins will have a positive nutritional effect on the children's academic performance. The working hypothesis and the null hypothesis must be *mutually exclusive* (when one is true the other must be false), so the experimenter's null hypothesis must be that vitamins will have no effect on the children's academic performance.

Imagine, now, two different sets of results of this experiment, results A and B as shown in Table 12.1. What conclusions would the researcher be willing to draw on the basis of results A as compared to results B?

In computing the means of these four groups, we find that the experimental groups of A and B have identical means ($\bar{X} = 15$) as do the control groups of A and B ($\bar{X} = 10$). Clearly, however,

TABLE 12.1
SIMPLE RANDOMIZED DESIGN WITH ALTERNATIVE RESULTS A AND B

Results A		Results B	
Vitamins	Control	Vitamins	Control
13	8	9	4
15	10	15	10
17	12	21	16

results A and B are different from one another. Within the conditions of results A the scores are more tightly bunched than they are in the conditions of results B. Notice, for example, that the three vitamin scores of results A (17, 15, 13) are all larger than are any of the three control group scores (12, 10, 8), while in results B the scores of the vitamin group (21, 15, 9) are more well-scrambled with the results of the control group (16, 10, 4). To put this in the technical vernacular introduced in Chapter 10, there is greater variability *within* each group in results B than within each group in results A.

When we compare the mean differences *between* the groups $[(\bar{X}_{exp} = 15) - (\bar{X}_{cont} = 10)]$, it would seem that we should also take into consideration these differences in variability. The 5 points of difference *between the groups* look larger to us when seen against the background of the small within-group variation of results A than against the background of the larger within-group variation of results B.

The most common method of comparing two means is to employ a statistic known as the t test, which tests the null hypothesis that there is in the population from which researchers have drawn their samples (*a*) no difference between the two means or (*b*) no relationship between the independent variable and the dependent variable. The t test is a test of significance that examines the difference between two means against the background of the within-group variability. The larger the difference between the means, and the smaller the within-group variability for any given size of experiment, the larger will be the t value (see Appendix for calculation of t).

Larger t values are thus associated with differences between means that are more "significantly different" from each other. That is to say, they have a lower level of probability that the differences might have occurred by chance. In this case, computing the t value in results A and then looking up the alpha level in a probability table would show an impressive probability ($p < .05$), but computing the t value in results B would show a poor probability ($p > .35$). In other words, there is only a very slim chance (1 in 20) in results A that the null hypothesis is true, but there is a pretty good chance (greater than 1 in 3) in results B that the null hypothesis is true. Results A, then, are much more impressive to researchers than are results B, if the researchers are hoping to find significant differences.

In planning their studies, researchers would like to maximize t by doing what they can to achieve significance. One way to maximize t would, of course, be to drive the means further apart. To do this, researchers need strong treatment effects which will produce large results in the experimental group as compared to the control. Another way to maximize t would be to decrease the variability within groups. This can be accomplished by standardizing the experimental conditions as much as possible and by employing more homogeneous samples of subjects. A third way to maximize t is to increase the size of the sample of subjects employed.

RANDOMIZED DESIGNS: THREE OR MORE CONDITIONS

The t test is useful whenever there are two groups to be compared, but some randomized designs are comprised of more than two groups. The term for research plans in which there are *two or more* groups to be compared on the dependent variable and in which the subjects are assigned to their group at random is a *fully randomized design*. In this case, a general test of significance is the F ratio, a test based on the *analysis of variance*, and the F ratio and t test are related to one another statistically (see Appendix). The simplest way to think of this relationship is that the t test is the square root of the F ratio when there are only two groups to be compared.

Let us look at another example to show how the reasoning is essentially the same in the use of the F ratio as in the t test. For our example, suppose that a researcher conducted an experiment on the effects of nutrition on the academic performance of ghetto children and used four groups rather than two. One group of randomly assigned children gets a hot lunch daily, another group gets free milk, a third group gets a vitamin supplement, and the fourth group gets nothing extra. Once again imagine two different sets of results of this experiment, represented by results A and B in Table 12.2.

Note that there are 12 subjects in each alternative set of results, and the subjects are assigned randomly and numbered arbitrarily from 1 to 12 for identification. Looking at these results, what conclusions would we be willing to draw on the basis of results A compared to results B? We note for both sets of results that the academic performance of the group receiving no special nutritional bonus (group I) was 10 units of academic performance, on the average (that is, $\bar{X}$ of group 1 = 10). Also, on the average, the group receiving milk (group II) scored 12 ($\bar{X}$ = 12), that receiving vitamins (group III) scored $\bar{X}$ = 15, while that receiving hot lunches scored $\overline{X} = 19$. Suppose we make a graph of these results to accentuate these differences, as shown in Figure 12.1.

This kind of pictorial display, called a *bar diagram* (or "bar graph" or "histogram"), is the most common type of figure for showing frequencies, percentages, or means for various subgroups. In this case, the data are grouped to show best the mean increases in academic performance as our eye moves from the results in the zero groups to the hot lunch groups. Since this bar diagram shows that the average performance of each of the four groups was the same for the two sets of results, will we not draw the same conclusions from both sets of results? Perhaps we would draw generally the same conclusion that hot lunches seem more effective than vitamins, which in turn are more effective than milk, which seems to be somewhat better than nothing.

However, following the logic of our analysis of the simple randomized design, when we go back to the actual raw scores (in Table 12.2) corresponding to these bars, we find ourselves feeling more impressed by results A than by results B. In results A, subjects never varied in their performance by more than 2 points from the average score of their group, while subjects in results B varied as much as 6 points from the average score of their group. The few points of difference between the mean scores of the four groups look larger when seen against the background of the small within-group variation of results A, while they look smaller when seen against the background of the large within-group variation of results B.

The analysis of variance provides researchers with a more

FIGURE 12.1
Bar diagram depicting the results shown in Table 12.2.

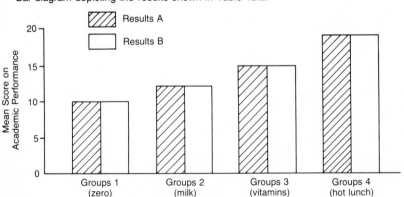

TABLE 12.2
FULLY RANDOMIZED DESIGN WITH ALTERNATIVE RESULTS A AND B

Alternative results A	Group 1 (zero)	Group 2 (milk)	Group 3 (vitamins)	Group 4 (hot lunch)
	$S_1 = 8$	$S_2 = 10$	$S_3 = 13$	$S_4 = 17$
	$S_5 = 10$	$S_6 = 12$	$S_7 = 15$	$S_8 = 19$
	$S_9 = 12$	$S_{10} = 14$	$S_{11} = 17$	$S_{12} = 21$
Alternative results B				
	$S_1 = 4$	$S_2 = 6$	$S_3 = 9$	$S_4 = 13$
	$S_5 = 10$	$S_6 = 12$	$S_7 = 15$	$S_8 = 19$
	$S_9 = 16$	$S_{10} = 18$	$S_{11} = 21$	$S_{12} = 25$

formal comparison of the variation between the average results per condition and the average variation within the different conditions. In such an analysis, a ratio (the F ratio) is formed with the variance of group means from one another multiplied by the number of scores in each of the conditions divided by the variance of individual scores from the means of their particular conditions. This ratio will have a value close to 1.0 when the variation between conditions is not different from the variation within conditions. The larger the F ratio becomes, the greater is the dispersion of group means relative to the dispersion of scores within groups. In other words, the larger the F ratio, the less likely it becomes that the dispersion among group means could easily have occurred by chance. In this particular case, the F ratio for results B is only one-ninth the size of the F ratio for results A in Table 12.2.

Statistical tables are available that show researchers for any particular F the probability (p) that an F of that size or larger might have been obtained by chance (i.e., if the null hypothesis were true). Reference to such a table in this case would show that results A could have occurred by chance less than five times in a thousand ($p < .005$), while results B could have occurred by chance very, very often.

FACTORIAL DESIGNS

Often it is possible to design experiments in such a way that a researcher can assess the effects of more than one variable in combination with one or more other variables. Such designs, in which each level of one dimension (or *factor*) is administered in combination with each level of another dimension, are *factorial designs*. For our example of a factorial design, we use the data just seen in results A of Table 12.2 but rearrange the design into a new two-dimensional design—see Table 12.3.

What have we gained by arraying the groups into a two-dimensional factorial design (milk × vitamins) rather than in just the one dimension comparing all four conditions? One advantage of the new configuration is that more of the subjects available for the experiment are able to contribute to the major comparisons of the experiment (milk versus no milk; vitamins versus no vitamins). Half of all the subjects of the experiment are in the milk condition instead of the quarter of all subjects that would be in the milk condition in a one-dimensional design. Thus half of the subjects can be compared to the remaining half of the subjects who received no milk, so that all the subjects of the experiment shed light on the question of the effect of milk. The effect of milk would be assessed in this case by a comparison of the milk and no milk *column means,* which for no milk is $\overline{X} = 12.5$ and for milk is $\overline{X} = 15.5$. At the same time that all subjects are providing information on the milk comparison, they are also contributing information on the effects of vitamins. The effect of vitamins would be assessed by a comparison of the no vitamins and vitamins *row means,* which with the same number of subjects are $\overline{X} = 11$ and $\overline{X} = 17$, respectively. That all subjects serve double duty is one of the great advantages of designs such as this. Each subject helps us to learn about the effect of columns while at the same time teaching us about the effect of rows.

Table 12.4 summarizes these means and N's and helps us to visualize the results a little better. It also helps us to see another

TABLE 12.3
TWO-DIMENSIONAL FACTORIAL DESIGN

		Milk	
		No	**Yes**
Vitamins	**No**	$S_1 = 8$ $S_5 = 10$ $S_9 = 12$	$S_2 = 10$ $S_6 = 12$ $S_{10} = 14$
	Yes	$S_3 = 13$ $S_7 = 15$ $S_{11} = 17$	$S_4 = 17$ $S_8 = 19$ $S_{12} = 21$

TABLE 12.4
SUMMARY OF MEANS AND THE NUMBER OF SUBJECTS (n OR N) FOR
DATA IN TABLE 12.3

	No milk	**Milk**	
No vitamins	Mean = 10 n = 3	Mean = 12 n = 3	Row mean = 11 n = 6
Vitamins	Mean = 15 n = 3	Mean = 19 n = 3	Row mean = 17 n = 6
	Column mean = 12.5 n = 6	Column mean = 15.5 n = 6	Grand Mean = 14 N = 12

advantage of this factorial design, which is that we can learn whether the effects of one of our dimensions, or factors, is much the same for each of the two or more conditions of the other factor. Looking at the means of the four conditions shows that there is a 2-unit effect ($12 - 10 = 2$) of milk when no vitamins are given but a 4-unit effect ($19 - 15 = 4$) of milk when vitamins are given. Similarly, there is a 5-unit effect ($15 - 10 = 5$) of vitamins when no milk is given but a 7-unit effect ($19 - 12 = 7$) of vitamins when milk is given. These differences between differences are termed *interaction effects,* and their probability of having occurred by chance (i.e., if the null hypothesis were true) can be evaluated by the methods of the analysis of variance referred to earlier (see Appendix for computational formulas).

Thus we see that the factorial design not only uses subjects more efficiently to answer questions, but is able to answer more questions than a one-dimensional design can. In the case of the fully randomized design, we asked one question: What is the overall effect of nutrition on academic performance? Now we see that it is possible to ask several more focused questions:

1 What is the effect on academic performance of daily milk?

2 What is the effect on academic performance of daily vitamins?

3a Is the effect of vitamins different when milk is also given compared to when milk is not given? or

3b Is the effect of milk different when vitamins are also given as compared to when vitamins are not given?

REPEATED-MEASURES DESIGNS

This third basic design can be seen as a special case of a two-dimensional design in which a number of experimental (or control) conditions are applied to each of a number of subjects. One dimension is the effect of the treatments, while the other dimension is the array (or grouping) of subjects. Because there is only a single score for each subject entered for each condition, there can be no estimate of within-condition variability. Table 12.5 illustrates the repeated-measures design for our four familiar treatment conditions each of which has been applied, a month at a time, to each of three different subjects.

Previously each of our sampling units was observed only once, but here we see that each subject was observed once a month for a total of four times. The design takes its name from the fact that each subject is observed or measured repeatedly; sometimes the very nature of the research question calls for this type of design. For example, if a researcher were interested in examining the effects of practice on the performance of a learning task, or the effects of age in a longitudinal study of development, it would seem natural to employ the same sampling units repeatedly over time. In the example shown in Table 12.5, it would be impossible to separate the effects of the treatments from the simple effects of time. That would require a more complex repeated-measures design in which the sequences of treatments were systematically varied to take into account the "confounding" of treatment with time. However, this simple example does serve to illustrate the logic of repeated-measures designs.

EFFECT SIZE

So far we have talked about significance testing, but we have not said anything about effect size in connection with t or F. We must emphasize, however, that the results of a study with respect to *any* given relationship can be expressed as an estimate of an effect size and a test of significance. The Pearson r is widely used, easily computed, and very general in applicability as a measure of

TABLE 12.5
REPEATED-MEASURES DESIGN

	January Condition 1 (zero)	February Condition 2 (milk)	March Condition 3 (vitamins)	April Condition 4 (hot lunch)
Subject 1	8	12	15	21
Subject 2	10	14	17	19
Subject 3	12	10	13	17

effect size. The reader interested in how r can be calculated from t or F will find formulas at the end of our discussion in the Appendix.

SUMMARY

A great many experimental designs are often found to be of value in behavioral research. Many of them are related to the designs presented here, so that an understanding of these general designs should make other designs more comprehensible on an intuitive level. The advantage of factorial designs is that they employ subjects more efficiently and address more research questions than do the simple or fully randomized designs discussed in this chapter. Sometimes the nature of the problem under investigation will call for repeated measures of subjects, which can be seen as a special case of a two-dimensional (factorial) design. Whatever design is used, the weight of the researcher's decision process with respect to the null hypothesis can be best expressed as an estimate of the effect size (for example, r) and a test of significance (for example, F or t).

KEY TERMS

analysis of variance (see Appendix)
bar diagram (histogram)
factor (dimension)
factorial designs
F ratio
fully randomized designs
interaction effect
repeated-measures designs
simple randomized design
t test

PART FIVE

LIMITS OF BEHAVIORAL RESEARCH

CHAPTER 13

ARTIFACTS IN BEHAVIORAL RESEARCH

Previously we defined the terms reactive and nonreactive to distinguish measurements or observations that do (*reactive*) from those that do not (*nonreactive*) affect the object being measured or observed. When an engineer carefully takes the dimensions of a large piece of metal, we do not suppose that the act of measurement will have an effect on the metal. Similarly, when a biologist observes the movements of a paramecium, we should not expect that the paramecium will behave much differently when the scientist is looking through the microscope than when the scientist is looking away from it. However, one may be less sure of the risks of reactive observation when primates are the object of study. Is the chimpanzee's behavior apt to be affected by its awareness of having captured the attentive interest of the behavioral scientist? With human subjects, of course, the problem of reactive observation is even more salient. The term used to refer to this specific threat to validity that is a result of the behavioral scientist's observations is an *artifact,* and in this chapter we shall consider two primary sources of artifacts, the subject and the experimenter.

DEMAND CHARACTERISTICS AND SUBJECT ARTIFACTS

One way of thinking about subject artifacts is in terms of what sociologists call "role theory." This theory, which was derived from the dramaturgical analogy of the human subject as an actor playing a role, asserts that a large part of human social behavior is guided by the wishes, expectations, and behavior of others. For the human research subject, it is recognized that he or she, no less than other socialized human beings, is sensitive to the wishes, expectations, and behavior of the other participants and the experimenter.

In an experiment, the objective is to observe behavior in a precisely controlled situation where the experimenter can manipulate the independent variable or interfere with some normally occurring relationship while holding other variables constant. To be able to draw valid inferences from the research findings that are generalizable to a comparable situation outside of the laboratory setting requires that the experimental conditions closely resemble the naturalistic processes under investigation. Insofar as the research subject is playing a different role than he or she would play in the corresponding naturalistic situation, it may be difficult to draw conclusions that can be generalized beyond the laboratory setting. This would have the effect of diminishing the external validity of the laboratory findings.

In fact, there are several roles that the subject might play. One is that of the *good subject*. The good subject's creed could be a paraphrase of the old song about Lola: "Whatever experimenters want, experimenters get." The good subject is excessively sensitive and accommodating to the experimenter's implicit wishes and expectations for the experimental outcome. Of course, not everyone is willing to play the good subject, although many volunteer subjects have been found to be quite willing to do whatever the experimenter asks of them.

Martin T. Orne (1962) has done extensive research into this type of role enactment. He has introduced the expression *demand characteristics of the experimental situation* to denote the mixture of various hints and cues that govern subjects' perceptions of their roles and of the experimenter's hypothesis. At one point in his research on hypnosis, Orne tried to devise a set of dull, meaningless tasks that he hoped the control subjects would either refuse to do or would try for a short time and abandon. One task was to add hundreds of thousands of 2-digit numbers until the experimenter told them to stop. Five-and-a-half hours after the subjects began, the experimenter gave up! The subjects never did quit.

Even when they were told to tear each individual sheet from a stack of completed arithmetic work sheets into no less than 32 pieces and then go on to the next and do the same thing, the subjects kept on working. Orne's (1962) explanation for this unusual behavior was that the subjects were reacting to demand characteristics in the context of the fact that they were research subjects. Feeling that they had a stake in the outcome of the experiment, they attributed meaning to an utterly meaningless task. It was as if they reasoned that no matter how inane the task might seem to others, the experimenter must surely have an important scientific purpose to justify asking them to work so energetically on seemingly trivial addition problems.

Some research participants are also described as *apprehensive subjects*, based on their apparent high need for social approval. Milton J. Rosenberg (1969) coined the term *evaluation apprehension* to characterize this "feeling state," which is highly conducive to a fear of being judged or evaluated. Such a subject will behave in a way so as to "look good" in the eyes of the experimenter. Looking good may mean complying with demand characteristics. But as Rosenberg and others have found, it can also mean *not* complying with demand characteristics if that is what is required to project a favorable image. Experimenters have reported that when there is a conflict between complying with demand characteristics and projecting a good appearance, most subjects will prefer to look good than to cooperate with demand characteristics (e.g., Rosnow, Goodstadt, Suls, & Gitter, 1973).

A third type of role motivation is that of the *negativistic subject*. This type approaches the experimental situation with an uncooperative and possibly hostile attitude. The negativistic subject is just the opposite of the good subject. Instead of going along with demand characteristics, the negativistic subject may do everything possible to ruin the experiment.

COPING WITH SUBJECT ARTIFACTS

In Chapter 7, we discussed the concept of *construct validity*. It is easy to see how subject artifacts resulting from a particular role enactment might be a threat to construct validity (in addition to external validity). For this reason it is always important that researchers consider the possibility that what one experimenter interprets as a causal relationship between X and Y may be seen by another researcher as the relationship between some role variable and Y (Cook & Campbell, 1979).

Various ways of coping with these potent threats to validity have been developed. We shall mention three strategies. Previously we discussed certain unobtrusive measurements, and one possibility for avoiding subject artifacts is to do field experiments using disguised measures. Because subjects are unaware that they are being scientifically studied, there is no reason for them to be sensitive to the demand characteristics of the situation.

An example of field experimentation using disguised measures was a cross-national research study on helping behavior that was conducted by Roy E. Feldman (1968). For many kinds of behavior, the cultural context in which the behavior is enacted can be an important independent variable. Feldman repeated several standard experiments in Athens, Paris, and Boston, using both foreigners and natives of the region as confederates or pseudosubjects. In one study, he had the pseudosubjects ask directions from passersby; in another, they asked strangers to mail a letter for them, explaining that they were waiting for someone and could not leave the spot right then; in a third study, pseudosubjects overpaid merchants or taxi drivers and observed whether the people were honest and returned the money. By cross-tabulating the results of the reactions of more than 3,000 research subjects, Feldman was able to show that when a difference in helping behavior occurred, Parisians and Bostonians treated compatriots better than they did foreigners while Athenians were more helpful to foreigners than to compatriots. The point is that the subjects, being unaware of the fact that they were participating in a psychological experiment, were not tempted to play an artificial role but instead behaved as they normally would in real life.

Another procedure for coping with subject artifacts is to use *quasi-control subjects* to detect demand characteristics (Orne, 1969). These are subjects drawn from the same population as the regular subjects, but who are asked to step out of their role of research subject and to serve as "co-investigators" rather than subjects for the experimenter to manipulate. Quasi-control subjects are told to reflect upon the context in which the particular experiment is being conducted and to speculate on ways in which demand characteristics might influence their behavior if they were participating in the experiment. Although these subjects never actually take part in the experiment, they are given the same information that regular subjects would be receiving.

A third procedure that is sometimes used is to observe the dependent variable more than once in different contexts. The objective is to tease out the effects of situational demand characteristics (Rosnow & Aiken, 1973). In a study by Orne and his colleagues, this procedure was used to detect the persistent effects of demand characteristics in an experiment on hypnosis. The hypnotized subjects and a control group of subjects who were told to simulate hypnosis were given the suggestion that, for the next two days, every time they heard the word "experiment" mentioned they would respond by touching their forehead (Orne, Sheehan, & Evans, 1968). Initially the researchers tested the suggestion in the original experimental setting. They then tested it when the situation was different. They had a secretary in the waiting room confirm the time of the subject's appointment "to come for the next part of the *experiment.*" Later she asked the subject if she could pay him "now for today's *experiment* and for the next part of the study tomorrow." On the following day she met the subject with the question: "Are you here for Dr. Sheehan's *experiment?*"

In this way it was possible repeatedly to observe the critical response both outside and inside the laboratory setting. Although the subjects were aware of being observed, Orne argues that we can safely assume that they did not connect the fact of being observed by the secretary with the demand characteristics of the experimental situation. In fact, no simulating subjects responded to the secretary's suggestion in the waiting room on both days, but 5 out of 17 hypnotized subjects did so. The results of this experiment, while not showing an overwhelmingly large effect, nevertheless support the hypothesis that posthypnotic behavior is not limited to the experimental setting.

NONINTERACTIONAL EXPERIMENTER EFFECTS

While some researchers have focused their attention on the subject's perceptions and reactions to demand characteristics, other researchers have been concerned with the types of artifacts that are attributable to the experimenter as a person or to the experimenter's behavior. One general category of experimenter effects includes any type of *noninteractional* artifacts, that is to say, experimenter effects that occur without affecting the actual response of the subject. A second general category includes any type of *interactional* artifacts, or effects that operate by influencing the actual response of the subject. We shall now give examples of these two general categories, beginning with two examples of the noninteractional variety.

One type of noninteractional experimenter effect is an *observer effect,* since the observer must make provision for the human limitations of accurate observation. This lesson was first taught to scientists by astronomers near the end of the eighteenth century. The royal astronomer at the Greenwich Observatory in England, a man named Maskelyne, discovered that his assistant, Kinnebrook, was consistently "too slow" in his observations of the movements of stars across the sky. Maskelyne cautioned Kinnebrook about his "errors," but the errors continued unabated for months. Kinnebrook was fired. Twenty years later, an astronomer at Königsberg, a man named Bessel, arrived at the conclusion that Kinnebrook's "error" was probably not willful, that is, different people perceive at different speeds. Bessel studied the observations of stellar transits made by a number of senior astronomers. Differences in observation, he discovered, were the rule, not the exception (Boring, 1950).

Kinnebrook's error was unintentional, but sometimes scientists intentionally falsify data (called an *intentional effect*). Such instances do, however, seem to be rare (Weinstein, 1979). Nevertheless, intentional effects must be regarded as part of the inventory of the effects of investigators themselves. Recently there was the case of the late Cyril Burt, whose work has been played up in the nature-nurture debate concerning the influence of heredity versus the environment on intelligence. In three separate reports of more than 20, more than 30, and more than 50 pairs of twins, Burt reported a correlation between IQ scores of those twins who had been raised apart that was identical to three decimal places for all three studies! Such consistency of correlation would bespeak a statistical miracle if it were true (Kamin, 1974).

Observer effects and intentional effects all operate without the experimenter's influencing the subject's actual response. A powerful, necessary, though insufficient tool for the control of these effects is our awareness of them. That some of these effects are fully public events ensures that in time they may be discovered by the addition of new observations through the process of replication.

INTERACTIONAL EXPERIMENTER EFFECTS

We now look at two examples of interactional effects, that is, experimenter effects that operate by affecting the actual response of the participant. The first is a *biosocial effect* of the experimenter, since it involves some combination of biological and sociological variables such as gender, age, and race. The second example, which we alluded to in previous chapters, is the *experimenter expectancy effect,* which operates like a "self-fulfilling prophecy" (Chapter 3 discussion).

When researchers refer to biosocial experimenter effects, they mean (*a*) that subjects may respond differently simply to the presence of experimenters varying in attributes such as gender, age, and race, or (*b*) that experimenters varying in these attributes behave differently toward their subjects and therefore obtain different responses. Thus far the evidence suggests that male and female experimenters may conduct the "same" experiment quite differently, so that the different results they obtain may well be due to the fact that they have unintentionally conducted different experiments. For example, male experimenters have been found to be more friendly to their subjects (Rosenthal, 1977).

Biosocial attributes of subjects can also affect the experimenter's behavior, which in turn affects the subjects' responses. In one study, the interactions between experimenters and their subjects were recorded on sound films. The study found that only 12 percent of the experimenters ever smiled at their male subjects, while 70 percent of the experimenters smiled at their female subjects. Smiling by the experimenters, it was also found, affected the results of the experiment (Rosenthal, 1967). The moral is clear. Before claiming a sex difference in the results of behavioral research, scientists must first be sure that males and females were treated identically by the experimenter. If they were not, then sex differences may be due not to constitutional or socialization factors, but simply to the fact that males and females did not in effect participate in the same experiment. That is, they were treated differently.

The experimenter expectancy effect, our second example of an interactional effect, is by far the best known of this class of artifacts. Some expectation of how the research will turn out is virtually a constant in science, and in this case, we are referring to the investigator's hypothesis as a self-fulfilling prophecy. The experimenter prophesies an event (the working hypothesis), and the expectation of this event then changes the behavior of the prophet (the experimenter) in such a way as to make the prophesied event more likely. The history of science documents the occurrence of this phenomenon with the "case of Clever Hans" as prime example.

EXPERIMENTER EXPECTANCY EFFECTS

Clever Hans was the horse of a man named Wilhelm von Osten (a German mathematics instructor) at the turn of this century. Von Osten claimed that Hans was able to "verbalize" difficult mathematical calculations as well as to spell, read, and solve problems of musical harmony simply by tapping his hoof. As it turned out, Hans was certainly "clever," but his cleverness was due to his ability to detect unintentional cues from his questioners rather than to his reputed ability to reason. Observers' postural movements were unconscious signals to Hans as to when to tap his hoof and when to stop. However, von Osten held to his anthropomorphic belief in the horse's rationality in the face of this adverse finding by a young psychologist of this period, Oskar Pfungst.

Pfungst, in a series of brilliant experiments, showed that Hans could answer questions only when the questioner or experimenter himself knew the answer and was within the horse's view. Pfungst learned that an unconscious forward movement of the experimenter's head was all the signal that Hans needed to start tapping. A tiny upward movement of the questioner's head or a raising of his eyebrows was the unconscious signal to Hans to stop his tapping. The questioners had *expected* Hans to give correct answers, and their expectancies were reflected in their unwitting signals to Hans to start and then to stop his tapping. Thus the questioner's expectation became the reason for the horse's amazing abilities.

Recent experiments have shown that an investigator's working hypothesis and expectations can also sometimes come to serve as self-fulfilling prophecies. In one study, a dozen undergraduate experimenters were each given five rats that were to be taught to run a maze. Half the experimenters were told their rats had been specifically bred for maze brightness; the remaining experimenters were told their rats had been bred for maze dullness. There were, of course, no actual differences between the rats assigned to each of those two groups. At the end of the experiment the results were clear. Rats that had been run by experimenters expecting brighter behavior showed significantly superior learning compared to rats run by experimenters expecting duller behavior (Rosenthal & Fode, 1963).

The experiment was replicated, this time using a series of learning trials, each conducted in Skinner boxes. Half the experimenters were led to believe their rats were "Skinner box bright" and half were led to believe their rats were "Skinner box dull." Once again there were not really any differences in the two groups of rats, at least not until the end of the experiment. Then, the allegedly brighter animals really were brighter, and the alleged dullards really were duller (Rosenthal & Lawson, 1964).

Among the strategies that can be used to reduce or control for the possibility of an experimenter expectancy effect are (*a*) increasing the number of experimenters (which increases generality of results by randomizing expectancies), (*b*) analyzing experiments for order effects (which permits inference about changes in experimenter behavior), (*c*) developing training procedures for experimenters (which permits prediction of expectancy effects), and (*d*) maintaining "blind contact" between experimenters and subjects (which minimizes expectancy effects). A particular strategy previously mentioned in Chapter 5 in our discussion of the logic of research designs is the *expectancy control design*, another variation of which is shown in Table 13.1.

In this design it will be recalled that the strategy is to allow the expectancy variable to operate separately from the independent variable in which the researcher is ordinarily most interested. Table 13.1 summarizes the results of a study of teachers' expectations for their pupils' success in learning to read (Palardy, 1969).

The research found two groups of teachers, one in which boys were expected to do as well as girls and one in which boys were expected to do less well than girls. The table shows that there was no difference in the reading achievement of boys and girls taught by teachers who expected no difference, but that boys did not do as well as girls in the classrooms of teachers who expected that boys would not do as well as girls.

SUMMARY

In this chapter, we examined two general categories of artifacts, or specific threats to validity, which are a result of the scientist's observations. One category of artifacts included those due to the subjects' responding to demand characteristics in the context of their own role motivations. Strategies for coping with this subject artifact included the use of field experiments and disguised mea-

TABLE 13.1
A VARIATION ON THE EXPECTANCY-CONTROL DESIGN

	Boys	Girls
Equal expectations for boys and girls	96.5	96.2
Lower expectations for boys than for girls	89.2	96.7

sures, quasi-control subjects in addition to regular controls, and multiple measurement of the dependent variable in different situations. The second category of artifacts included those due to interactional and noninteractional experimenter effects. Best known of the interactional variety is the experimenter expectancy effect, which operates like a self-fulfilling prophecy and can be teased out by the use of an expectancy control design.

KEY TERMS

apprehensive subject
artifact
biosocial effect
demand characteristics of the experimental situation
evaluation apprehension
experimenter expectancy effect
good subject
intentional effect
interactional experimenter effect (versus noninteractional)
negativistic subject
observer effect
quasi-control subject

CHAPTER 14

ETHICAL CONDUCT OF RESEARCH

By *ethics* we mean the system of moral values or standards by which the members of a society live. In behavioral science, there are a number of such systems that have been developed by professional organizations for the purpose of regulating the conduct of human subject research. In this chapter, we deal with the nature of particular values or standards and their implications for individual researchers who must weigh their responsibilities to science as well as to society.

OPENNESS IN RESEARCH

Imagine an experiment in which the experimenter greeted the subjects by saying, "Hello, today we are going to investigate the effects of physical distance from the victim on willingness to inflict pain on him. You will be in the 'close' condition, which means that you are expected to be somewhat less ruthless. In addition, you will be asked to fill out a test of fascist tendencies because we believe there is a positive relationship between scores on our fascism test and obedience to an authority who requests that we hurt others. Any questions?"

A completely honest statement to a research subject of what he or she is doing in an experiment might involve a briefing of this kind. Such a briefing would be manifestly absurd in this case if we were serious in our efforts to learn about human behavior. In other cases as well, however, if subjects had full information about scientists' experimental plans, procedures, and hypotheses, we might very well develop a science based on what subjects thought the world was like or what subjects thought experimenters thought the world was like. Subjects' awareness of demand characteristics, coupled with their tendency to want to be "good subjects" or to "look good" in the eyes of the experimenter, constitutes a special case of reactive observation (as we learned in the preceding chapter).

The problem of subjects' knowledge of the true intent of the experiment is sufficiently threatening to the validity (internal, external, construct) of the research that behavioral scientists have, in many cases, routinely employed one form or another of *active* or *passive deception* of subjects. For example, Arellano-Galdames (1972) mentions the following kinds of active deception (deception by commission):

1 Misrepresentation of the purpose of the investigation.
2 Untrue statements about the identity of the researcher.
3 False promises.
4 Violation of the promise of anonymity.
5 Incorrect explanations of equipment and procedures.
6 Use of confederates (pseudosubjects).
7 Use of placebos and secret application of medications and drugs.

On the other hand, there are also passive deception procedures (deception by omission):

1 Concealed observation.
2 Provocation and secret recording of negatively evaluated behavior.
3 Unrecognized participant observation.
4 Use of projective techniques and other personality tests.
5 Unrecognized conditioning of subjects' behaviors.

There are very few behavioral and social scientists who would advocate the use of deception for its own sake. At the same time, there are few researchers who feel that behavioral or social science can do entirely without some of the deception practices mentioned above. No social scientist would seriously advocate giving up the study of prejudice and discrimination. Yet if all measures of prejudice and discrimination had to be accurately labeled as such, it is questionable that it would be worth the effort to continue this research.

To adopt a rigid moralistic orientation requires that a deception be labeled a deception and that by our dominant value system (which decries deception, at least in a formal sense) it be banished or ruled out. In fact, most people, behavioral scientists included, are willing to weigh and measure their sins, judging some to be larger than others. In the case of deceptions, fairly good agreement could probably be obtained on the proposition that refraining from telling a subject that an experiment in the learning of verbal materials is designed to show whether "earlier, later, or intermediate material is better remembered" is not a particularly serious breach of ethical standards. The reason most behavioral scientists do not view this deception with alarm seems, on first glance, due in part to its involving a "sin of omission" (passive deception) rather than "commission" (active deception). A truth is left unspoken; a lie is not told.

Suppose, however, that the same experiment were presented as a study of the "effects of meaningfulness of verbal material on retention or recall." That is a direct lie (active deception), designed to mislead the subject's attention from the temporal order of the material to some other factor in which the scientist is really not interested. But somehow, that change does not seem to make the deception so much more heinous even though now the sin is one of commission and the scientist has not withheld information from, but actively lied to, the subject.

PROBABLE EFFECT OF DECEPTIONS

It does not seem, then, that the active or passive style of a deception is its measure; instead, its probable effect on the subject is what is significant. Very few people would care whether subjects focused on meaningfulness of verbal material rather than temporal order, since there seems to be no consequence (positive or negative) of this deception. It seems that it is not deception so much as it is harmful deception that we would like to minimize, and that it is the degree of harmfulness on which researchers may agree fairly well.

Most researchers, for example, would probably agree that it is not very harmful to subjects to be told that a test they are taking anonymously as part of the research is one of personal reactions (which it is) rather than a test of need for social approval, schizophrenic tendencies, or authoritarianism (which it may also be). On the other hand, most researchers would probably agree that it could be harmful to college age subjects to be falsely told that a test shows them to be homosexual even if they are later told that they had been misled.

Some of the potentially most harmful deceptions, perhaps, ought never to be employed, but then they are quite rare in any case. For the great bulk of deceptions where there may be a range of potentially negative consequences, the investigator, colleagues, and to some extent, ultimately, the general community, must decide whether a deception of a given degree of potential negative effects is worth the potential increase in knowledge. There has been some interest in demonstrating empirically the ethical dilemma that confronts the behavioral scientist who on the one hand wishes to be open and straightforward with the research subjects, while on the other hand realizing that the validity of his or her findings could be called into question. By revealing the substance of the research to participating subjects, the experimenter could be clouding the findings by introducing artifacts.

AN EXAMPLE

A study that illustrates this point was that done by Jerome H. Resnick and Thomas Schwartz (1973). The objective of this study was to document the experimental effects of *informed consent,* that is, informing the potential subjects of the nature of the research and then requesting their consent to participate. The particular procedure used by Resnick and Schwartz was mentioned in Chapter 3, and involved a verbal conditioning method in which the experimenter shapes the subject's utterances by saying "Good" or "Mm-hmm" or "Okay" every time the subject gives the desired verbal response.

In Resnick and Schwartz's study, the subject and the experimenter were seated at opposite sides of a table across which the experimenter passed a series of 3 x 5 inch cards to the subject one at a time. A different verb and six pronouns (I, we, you, they, she, he) were printed on each card. The subject's instructions were to construct a sentence containing the verb and any one of the six pronouns. By rewarding the subject with verbal approval each time a sentence was begun with "I" or "we," the experimenter could observe the rate at which the subject learned to make these responses.

To provide a baseline for data analysis (by which to gauge how well each subject was progressing), on the first 20 trials the experimenter remained silent. In this way, subjects, by revealing what their usual standard of verbal behavior was like when the experimenter was not trying to condition them, could serve as their own controls when the verbal conditioning trials were started. These verbal conditioning trials (of which there were 80) followed immediately upon completion of the 20 baseline trials. To determine the effects of informed consent, the subjects were randomly assigned to either of two groups. In one group (the informed consent treatment), the experimenter was completely open with them on the purpose, explicit procedure, and expected results of the study. In the other group (the control group), he was not; the only information these subjects received concerned the general format of the experimental procedure.

Resnick and Schwartz's findings may not come as a surprise. For the uninformed (control) group, the conditioning results were exactly what other investigators had shown time and again. In effect, the experimenter's use of verbal reinforcements tended to facilitate the construction of I and we sentences. This finding is exactly what hundreds of other studies had reported and is part of the basis of behavioral science's current laws of verbal learning. For the informed consent group the results were just the opposite, however. Instead of playing the good subject, these subjects responded counter to demand characteristics. Several of them mentioned afterward that they suspected an elaborate "cover-up" and "double-reverse manipulation!"

Imagine what a science of verbal conditioning would look like if this prebriefing procedure were routinely used, or if it had been routinely used in those hundreds of verbal conditioning studies. Resnick and Schwartz's study emphasizes the complexity of the ethical conflict that faces behavioral scientists. The researcher is confronted with a genuine dilemma of values where he or she must weigh the humane ethic of informed consent against the scientific ethic of validity and decide which ought to carry the greater weight.

ETHICAL GUIDELINES

There are specific guidelines to which behavioral scientists can turn in helping them to reach a reasoned decision. Both in the United States and abroad, various professional organizations in the field of psychology (and other disciplines) have developed "codes of ethics" (or ethical guidelines) for the conduct of human subjects research (for discussion, see Schuler, 1982). To give one example, the American Psychological Association in 1983 published a set of 10 ethical guidelines emphasizing certain human guarantees that ought to weigh in psychologists' considerations as to how best to contribute to science and to human welfare.

The APA code recognizes that in each case there are balancing considerations for and against research that raises ethical issues. The code also recognizes that researchers may not be the most objective judges of the pros and cons of their own research when it raises an ethical question. Because personal involvement can blind even a very conscientious researcher, the code advises researchers to consult with others on their individual responsibilities. Following is the list of these 10 principles:*

The decision to undertake research rests upon a considered judgment by the individual psychologist about how best to contribute to psychological science and human welfare. Having made the decision to conduct research, the psychologist considers alternative directions in which research energies and resources might be invested. On the basis of this consideration, the psychologist carries out the investigation with respect and concern for the dignity and welfare of the people who participate and with cognizance of federal and state regulations and professional standards governing the conduct of research with human participants.

A. In planning a study, the investigator has the responsibility to make a careful evaluation of its ethical acceptability. To the extent that the weighing of scientific and human values suggests a compromise of any principle, the investigator incurs a correspondingly serious obligation to seek ethical advice and to observe stringent safeguards to protect the rights of human participants.

B. Considering whether a participant in a planned study will be a "subject at risk" or a "subject at minimal risk," according to recognized standards, is of primary ethical concern to the investigator.

C. The investigator always retains the responsibility for ensuring ethical practice in research. The investigator is also responsible for the ethical treatment of research participants by collaborators, assistants, students, and employees, all of whom, however, incur similar obligations.

D. Except in minimal-risk research, the investigator establishes a clear and fair agreement with research participants, prior to their participation, that clarifies the obligations and responsibilities of each. The investigator has the obligation to honor all promises and commitments included in that agreement. The investigator informs the participants of all aspects of the research that might reasonably be expected

---

to influence willingness to participate and explains all other aspects of the research about which the participants inquire. Failure to make full disclosure prior to obtaining informed consent requires additional safeguards to protect the welfare and dignity of the research participants. Research with children or with participants who have impairments that would limit understanding and/or communication requires special safeguarding procedures.

E. Methodological requirements of a study may make the use of concealment or deception necessary. Before conducting such a study, the investigator has a special responsibility to (1) determine whether the use of such techniques is justified by the study's prospective scientific, educational, or applied value; (2) determine whether alternative procedures are available that do not use concealment or deception; and (3) ensure that the participants are provided with sufficient explanation as soon as possible.

F. The investigator respects the individual's freedom to decline to participate in or to withdraw from the research at any time. The obligation to protect this freedom requires careful thought and consideration when the investigator is in a position of authority or influence over the participant. Such positions of authority include, but are not limited to, situations in which research participation is required as part of employment or in which the participant is a student, client, or employee of the investigator.

G. The investigator protects the participant from physical and mental discomfort, harm, and danger that may arise from research procedures. If risks of such consequences exist, the investigator informs the participant of that fact. Research procedures likely to cause serious or lasting harm to a participant are not used unless the failure to use these procedures might expose the participant to risk of greater harm or unless the research has great potential benefit and fully informed and voluntary consent is obtained from each participant. The participant should be informed of procedures for contacting the investigator within a reasonable time period following participation should stress, potential harm, or related questions or concerns arise.

H. After the data are collected, the investigator provides the participant with information about the nature of the study and attempts to remove any misconceptions that may have arisen. Where scientific or humane values justify delaying or withholding this information, the investigator incurs a special responsibility to monitor the research and to ensure that there are no damaging consequences for the participant.

I. Where research procedures result in undesirable consequences for the individual participant, the investigator has the responsibility to detect and remove or correct these consequences, including long-term effects.

J. Information obtained about a research participant during the course of an investigation is confidential unless otherwise agreed upon in advance. When the possibility exists that others may obtain access to such information, this possibility, together with the plans for protecting confidentiality, is explained to the participant as part of the procedure for obtaining informed consent.

COSTS AND UTILITIES

In the United States, almost all research institutions have established their own review panels (*institutional review boards*) to oversee the conduct of research guided by principles such as those listed above. In analyzing the morality of research with human subjects, these boards typically proceed on the basis of a conceptual model like the one depicted in Figure 14.1.

In this model, the "cost of doing" includes possible harm to subjects, time, expenditures of money, effort, etc., and the "utility of doing" includes benefits to subjects, to other people at other times and places, to the investigator, etc. Studies with high internal and external validity are more useful than studies with unacceptable validity standards, and studies addressing important issues are more useful than studies addressing trivial issues. Studies falling at point A *are not* carried out, while studies at point D *are* carried out. Studies falling along the diagonal of indecision, B–C, are so hard to decide about that they clearly call for modifications.

In recent years, however, it has been argued that this *decision-plane model* of the costs and utilities of doing research is insufficient. The insufficiency stems from its failure to delineate the costs (and utilities) of *not* conducting a particular study. The failure to conduct a study that could be conducted is as much an act to be evaluated on ethical grounds as is the conducting of a study. The oncologist who could find a cancer preventive but feels the work to be dull and a distraction from his or her real interests is making a decision that is to be evaluated on ethical

FIGURE 14.1
A model that represents the costs and utilities of doing research.

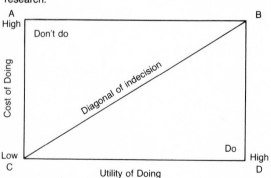

grounds as surely as the decision of a researcher to investigate tumors with a procedure that carries some risk. The behavioral scientist whose study might reduce violence or prejudice, but who refuses to do the study because it involves deception or violates standards of informed consent, has not solved the ethical problem but only traded one problem for another.

The model thus requires a balancing of considerations based on a more complete analysis of the costs and utilities of *doing* and *not doing* a study. However, even with this more complete analysis, behavioral scientists are also faced with the problem that the very nature of their research often challenges or questions a society's values and elicits emotional responses. When scientists describe certain behaviors as being normative, the implication to the layperson is that they are saying that such behaviors are to be expected and therefore desirable. When they study prejudice or mental illness, they are touching on highly charged social problems. Even when they study topics that may appear to them to be neutral (marriage and the family, social learning behavior, etc.), they realize that to others these topics may be supercharged with values and conflicts.

TREADING ON THIN ICE

It has been suggested that behavioral scientists should openly acknowledge that their work forces them to tread on "thin ice," morally speaking (Atwell, 1981). In studying social behavior, for instance, researchers are constantly in jeopardy of violating someone's basic right, if only the right of privacy.

There is another side to this problem that constantly confronts behavioral scientists. Each researcher must weigh how values enter into science not only in the ethics of the profession, but also in the selection of problems for scientific investigation. Even when research is not directly funded by some agency of society, it is at least countenanced and indirectly supported because our society places a high value on science and gives scientists a relatively free hand to study whatever they want to study. The question for scientists, then, is what do they owe society in return for this privilege?

Some scientists would answer that the behavioral scientist owes society the assurance that the research will lead to the betterment of humankind. This position is widely heralded especially during periods of social stress, when the clarion call is sounded for scientists to get out of their ivory towers and to formulate hypotheses that will be relevant to social problems. However, no scientist can guarantee the outcome of his or her work. Even the best motives can produce results that do not further the state of well-being for which scientists strive. What scientists can *try to do* is to protect the integrity of their work in order to ensure that it measures up to the standards of good scientific practice, and at the same time to respect both the dignity of those they study and the values that allow them to pursue scientific knowledge in a free society.

SUMMARY

The moral standards by which human subject research is judged necessarily impose restrictions on what is ethically permissible in behavioral science. Nevertheless, the model commonly used in making a cost-utility analysis is insufficient when it fails to consider the costs (and utilities) of *not* conducting a study. Moral standards also have implications for various technical scientific issues, such as the use of deception in research (discussed in this chapter) and the volunteer subject problem (discussed in Chapter 9). As a consequence, behavioral scientists must weigh their moral responsibilities both to science and to society.

KEY TERMS

cost of research
deception in research (active, passive)
decision-plane model (of costs and utilities)
diagonal of indecision
ethics
informed consent
institutional review boards
openness in research
utility of research

CHAPTER 15

TOWARD WIDER HORIZONS

In this chapter, our discussion comes full circle as we return to the concept of a regulative principle, an idea introduced in the opening chapter. As noted earlier, this is the philosophical notion that asserts that there are "hidden assumptions" that are not subject to empirical corroboration but nevertheless influence how researchers approach and attempt to comprehend the nature of empirical relations. One such principle is the *mechanistic position,* which likens human nature to a machine and regards human relations in terms of a push-and-pull mechanism that stresses action by contact. We shall explore the limitations of this position and how it has been challenged by a growing pluralistic revolution. In particular it has been challenged by the *contextualist position,* which (as we shall see) is a nonmechanistic alternative that provides a quite different way of looking at human relations.

THE MECHANISTIC POSITION

Briefly, in the late nineteenth century, spurred on by extraordinary successes in physics and chemistry, a number of leading researchers attempted to develop a philosophical model of mechanistic natural science as a way of tidying up the clutter of the subjective study of human behavior. Twentieth-century psychology developed in large part out of such a pronaturalist or naturalistic idealization, as did some other fields of behavioral science. Leading researchers in these fields had been inspired by the idea that the human system, like the physical systems of Galileo, Newton, and their intellectual predecessors, operated in a world of events running in a predictable mechanism of causes and effects. It followed that such a "machine" ought to be subject to causal laws (discussed in Chapter 2), so that under rigorous scientific conditions, definite relations could be isolated, predicted, and reproduced (replicated). The idea was even circulated that the experimental study of human behavior could proceed with the same disinterested curiosity with which physicists studied the refraction of light and chemists studied the properties of substances and elementary forms of matter. In this extreme view, value judgments, the distinction between "good" and "bad," and personal feelings had no place in science, which instead was idealized by many researchers as an instrument of defining *everything* in quantitative materialistic terms.

Give a small child a hammer and the child will find that everything needs pounding. The "law of the instrument" (Kaplan, 1964) helps us to understand much of behavioral science's obsession with this idea that was planted during the most formative years of its development. Coming along as it did in the heyday of the Industrial Revolution, the mechanistic position (with its emphasis on objective, value-free, universal laws, based on the assumption of external causes acting on effects) was an intoxicating idea for empiricists who were seeking credible scientific ways of addressing questions that had puzzled armchair theorizers since antiquity.

Modern philosophers of science (such as Thomas Kuhn and Stephen Pepper) refer to global views such as the mechanistic position as "world hypotheses" or "paradigms of science" (Kuhn, 1962; Pepper, 1942). They mean by this that the mechanical position is a conceptual schema that attempts to define the underpinnings, or prerequisites, of "normal science" in a given field. In previous chapters, we have alluded to how some of these underpinnings have been undermined by the artifact work and by questions directed at the ethics of certain "normal" practices in behavioral science. We now briefly review those discussions in the context of the traditional mechanistic claim regarding the objectivity and moral neutrality of behavioral science.

THE ARTIFACT ASSAULT

In Chapter 13, we discussed the work on artifacts in behavioral research, which first raised questions about the possibility that studying human behavior might be limited by reactive observations that imposed uncertainties on the behavior observed. The very act of measuring human behavior might, it was argued, negate the possibility of observing some human events as they would have occurred had they not been observed (Lana, 1969; Rosenzweig, 1933, Sarbin, 1944).

However, it was not until the 1960s—with the decline of methodological behaviorism (see Chapter 1)—that much of behavioral science became overtly receptive to the possibility that subjects' cognitions about the purposes of behavioral research might influence their behavior in the lab in ways unforeseen by investigators. Such a stance would presumably have been inconsistent with behaviorism's strict emphasis on only those things that can be directly observed and measured. Yet even behaviorists often used deceptions in their research, thus showing some implicit awareness of the issue of contamination by subject-artifacts.

The artifact work knocked the bottom out of the mechanistic position's view that human behavior could be studied in the way that chemists studied the properties of substances. In laying claim to the status of behavioral research as a natural science, some early researchers had failed to take fully into account the wider implications of studying a conscious human being within a social setting. On the basis of the artifact work, it appeared that researchers had a lower or smaller measure of control over the circumstances of their lab experiments as a result of systematic errors that derived from the conduct and context of human subject research, than they had formerly believed. Now it seemed that behavioral researchers were working with "dirty test tubes," or not with test tubes and substances at all.

One researcher discussed the essentially relativistic and ambiguous criteria that led to certain variables being called "artifacts"—since much of this research was itself based on lab experiments (McGuire, 1969). He proposed that there was a natural progression in the life of an artifact consisting of three stages. In the first stage, the researchers seemed ignorant of the variable producing the artifact and denied its existence when the possibility was pointed out to them. In the second stage, which began as the artifact's existence and possible importance became undeniable, the researchers gave a great deal of attention to developing ways of coping with its potential contaminating influence. In the third stage, they became interested in the artifact as a theoretical concept in its own right, not as a nuisance variable to be eliminated but as an independent variable with interesting possibilities for revealing new insights about human potentialities. By the late 1960s, it was clear that much of behavioral science had passed out of the ignorance stage and had entered the coping and exploitation stages.

Over the following decade, the concept of an artifact entered the mainstream of psychology and the research on artifacts (whatever its own failings) became common knowledge. This is not to say that the use of artifact controls (such as those discussed in Chapter 13) was necessarily widespread, but that the problem by this time had entered into the thinking of most investigators. However, even as researchers were learning of ways to cope with the artifact problem, the assumption of the moral neutrality of behavioral research was attacked.

THE VALUE ASSAULT

In the preceding chapter, we discussed questions having to do with the ethical conduct of human subject research. In the early development of behavioral science, it was often assumed that, just as a machine is amoral by its very nature, so must behavioral research (with its roots in mechanistic natural science) be value-free to preserve the ideal of objectivity. Some writers, on the other hand, attempted to draw a distinction between the natural and the behavioral sciences; they contended that the subject matter in the behavioral sciences made it more difficult to maintain scientific detachment. The subject matter of the natural sciences could be more easily viewed with ethical detachment or neutrality, they argued, in that it did not have concerns about human beings at its core.

As we all know, this distinction disappeared with the development of atomic physics and the atom bomb. Since that time there have been many questions raised about the moral implications of some of the most basic research in both the natural and behavioral sciences. It was because of such questions that professional associations, such as the American Psychological Association and others, have developed guidelines and codes for the ethical conduct of research (see Chapter 14).

The artifact assault taught researchers that their research was more human and subjective than many had perhaps believed. The value assault demolished illusions about the moral neutrality of behavioral science. These developments also paved the way for further assaults on the mechanistic position and have led to interesting new developments that have only just begun to unfold.

THE CONTEXTUALIST POSITION

One such development is an essentially nonmechanistic alternative, the *contextualist position*. The contextualist attempts to understand behavior in terms of the particular situation in which it occurs. Where, when, and before whom behavior is performed is no less significant than the universal causal agents that mechanists attempt to study, the contextualist would argue. Like a statement or message that makes complete sense only within the total context in which it occurs, much human behavior (according to this argument) is also comprehensible only as part of a context of social experiences that influence (and are influenced by) the behavior in question (cf. McGuire, 1983; Rosnow, 1981, 1983; among others).

There are several specific ways in which the mechanistic position and the contextualist position differ, though both agree on one basic assumption. Empirical confrontation is essential for refining the meaning and validity of scientific propositions. Mechanists emphasize the importance of research in terms of the confirmation of hypotheses and the *justification* of empirical assertions; contextualists emphasize that research is a *discovery* process to make clear the situational limitations of empirical relationships. Contextualists take the position that even contradictory theories about human nature can be valid under the "closed-off" circumstances assumed by the theories. Hence, the purpose of research is not to test whether theories are true (the mechanistic position) but instead to discover the contexts in which each theory adequately represents our observations (McGuire, 1983; Rosnow, 1978).

There are other characteristics of the contextualist position as an empirical scientific enterprise. First, contextualists concern themselves as much with *final causes* (which refer to the end reasons for which behavior seems naturally to aspire or strive; also called the "teleologic factor") as do mechanists with *efficient causes* (that is, the propelling factor that produces the behavior or sets it into motion or changes it). Second, given this concern with teleologic ends, contextualists also draw a distinction between "reasons" and "causes." Reasons are the justifications for behavior, while causes are the largely automatic or mechanical propellants of behavior. Third, contextualists tend (more than mechanists) to emphasize the *active,* volitional aspects of behavior as opposed to the purely mechanistic or *reactive* aspects. Fourth, contextualists are also very interested in the *processes* of behavior (the unfolding or evolution of behavior), while mechanists usually are more interested in the *products* of behavior as measured by one-shot questionnaires, experiments, etc.

PLURALISM IN BEHAVIORAL SCIENCE

So far we have painted a very extreme picture of behavioral scientists as mechanists *or* contextualists, when in fact life is not usually black and white but mostly gray. Recognizing that either extreme view is limited in some ways (in the same way that contextualists argue that theories are "closed-off"), one might say they are both *closed positions* in that they are specifically circumscribed by characteristics that seem to set a decisive limit to their fields of application (Rosnow, 1981, 1983).

For example, many of the methods that behavioral researchers prefer to use take a look at behavior only at a single point in time. They are *synchronic methods,* in that they are primarily concerned with the behavior in the here and now. The hidden assumption seems to be that behavior, being mechanistic, is like any other behavior at any other time and place. Contextualists, on the other hand, tend to favor *diachronic methods,* that is, methods that examine the unfolding of the behavior over time. In this case, the assumption seems to be that behavior, because it depends on reasons and purposes, may not have the same meaning in one situation as opposed to another, even though the behavior may superficially be similar.

Clearly there is much to be said for both of these positions. Perhaps you can think of some examples of purely mechanistic and contextualist types of behavior and experiences. Thus it might be said that either position by itself represents only part of the whole picture of human reality. Better than either view would be a more *pluralistic* view that attempted to comprehend behavior in terms of both its contexts and mechanics. Some believe that behavioral science is now experiencing an "identity crisis" much like the crisis experienced in physics.

The word "crisis," from the Greek *krisis,* meaning a division or separation, implies a crucial turning point. Such a point in the development of modern physics came about when a fundamental principle of classical mechanics—asserting that each physical system could be localized in space and time—was questioned. The uncertainty that followed when it was realized that the psychological subjective feeling of space and time was an invention of the mind and not (as Newton and others had assumed) something "absolute" possessing an independent existence, bred further confusion about other fundamental concepts and propositions. The resolution of this crisis of confidence—which led to a reconceptualization of space and time—ultimately resulted in a shifting of paradigms rather than in a negation of the mechanistic position.

In physics, this condition was crucial for preparing the way for the development of new paradigms by which it was then possible to redefine the field of natural science. Many researchers in behavioral science wonder whether recent developments challenging the mechanistic position in their field will also lead to a redefinition of the field. Whether it will, or whether the field might become more pluralistic in orientation, is something only time will tell.

SUMMARY

Throughout the earlier chapters of this book we examined how behavioral scientists have *usually* approached the study of human experience. The thrust of this approach in much of behavioral science has been traditionally based on a paradigm emphasizing the mechanics of behavior. Recently there has been a concerted challenge directed against this position and an apparent shift toward a more pluralistic science of behavior. The effects of this revolutionary change have only just begun to reverberate, making behavioral science a very exciting field at the present time. It remains to be seen whether these effects will produce a profound paradigm shift, a new synthesis along the lines of that which occurred in other scientific fields, or whether they will be subjugated by adherents to the status quo only to become the rallying cry for revolutions yet to come.

KEY TERMS

active versus reactive behavior
closed position
contextualist position
diachronic methods
efficient cause
final cause (teleologic factor)
law of the instrument
mechanistic position
moral neutrality
pluralism
synchronic methods
world hypothesis (paradigm)

APPENDIX: CRUNCHING NUMBERS

In Chapters 10 to 12, we introduced the conceptual side of the analysis of data, and in this appendix, we add some notes on the computation of three statistical procedures previously discussed, r, F, and t. We shall also say something about chi-square (χ^2) and the analysis of frequency counts in tables, which we feel to be useful even though in this brief discussion we can only be introductory in our exposition. While the earlier chapters were intended for readers with only the briefest acquaintance with quantitative methods, this appendix may be more of interest as an elementary introduction to data analysis for the number-crunchers among our readers.

COMPUTING r

We begin with the computation of the Pearson r (discussed in Chapter 11). We take for our illustration a case in which r was used to establish the *intercoder reliability* of two observers of teachers' warmth. Table A.1 shows some hypothetical ratings in such a check on observer reliability. The two observers, X and Y, rated nine teachers on warmth in the classroom on a scale that ranged from a score of 5 for maximum warmth to a 1 for minimum warmth.

TABLE A.1
SOME HYPOTHETICAL RATINGS OF TEACHERS' WARMTH BY TWO
OBSERVERS: PEARSON r

Teachers Rated	Observer X	Observer Y	X^2	Y^2	XY
a	5	4	25	16	20
b	5	3	25	9	15
c	4	5	16	25	20
d	4	4	16	16	16
e	4	3	16	9	12
f	3	3	9	9	9
g	3	1	9	1	3
h	2	2	4	4	4
i	1	2	1	4	2
$N = 9$	$\Sigma X = 31$	$\Sigma Y = 27$	$\Sigma X^2 = 121$	$\Sigma Y^2 = 93$	$\Sigma XY = 101$

The computational formula for the Pearson correlation is:

$$r = \frac{N(\Sigma XY) - (\Sigma X)(\Sigma Y)}{\sqrt{[N(\Sigma X^2) - (\Sigma X)^2][N(\Sigma Y^2) - (\Sigma Y)^2]}}$$

where N = number of X and Y pairs of ratings
X = any rating by observer X
Y = any rating by observer Y
Σ = summation sign, a mathematical symbol directing us to obtain the sum of a set of values

Substituting in this formula the values from Table A.1 gives us the following:

$$r = \frac{9(101) - (31)(27)}{\sqrt{[9(121) - (31)^2][9(93) - (27)^2]}}$$

$$= \frac{909 - 837}{\sqrt{(128)(108)}}$$

$$= \frac{72}{117.58}$$

$$= .61$$

Hence, for these two observers the correlation between their ratings was +.61, a value that, while not very close to 1.00, nevertheless is adequate for such global ratings of real-life behavior.

For any particular value of r we can look up its statistical significance in a table (e.g., Rosenthal & Rosnow, 1984), or we can compute a *t* test to assess the significance (or probability) that an *r* of that size might have occurred by chance (i.e., if *r* were really zero). We solve for *t* in the following:

$$t = \frac{r \sqrt{N - 2}}{\sqrt{1 - r^2}}$$

and then look up the *p* value associated with *t* in a table such as the sample listing of *t* values in Table A.2, which gives the *t* values that are required to reach any one of a number of levels of *p*. A larger *t* value (compared to a smaller one) is associated with a difference between means, or a difference between an obtained *r* and zero, that is more "significantly different" and has, therefore, a lower level of *p*, or probability, that the difference might have arisen by chance. The left-hand column of the table gives values of the quantity *N*−2, also known as the *degrees of freedom* (*df*) for *t*, which reflects the *size of the study* (that is, the number of observations). The general relationship between any test of significance (such as *t* or *F*) and the effect size (e.g., *r*) can be stated as:

Significance test = Effect size × Size of the study

which tells us that (given any particular effect size) for any test such as *t* or *F* to achieve significance at a given level (say, *p* = .05), we will need to make a certain minimal number of observations or use a certain minimal number of participants. In this case, if the *t* we were computing were based on two groups of three subjects each, our *N* = 6 and *N* − 2 = 4. As the sample listing of *t* values shows, smaller values of *t* are required to reach the same

TABLE A.2
SAMPLE LISTING OF *t* VALUES

N-2	Probability levels [a]			
	.10	.05	.01	.005
4	2.13	2.78	4.60	5.60
8	1.86	2.31	3.36	3.83
16	1.75	2.12	2.92	3.25
40	1.68	2.02	2.70	2.97
∞	1.64	1.96	2.58	2.81

[a] These *p* levels are "two-tailed," i.e., they apply regardless of whether the obtained *t* was positive or negative in sign. To make a one-tailed test, e.g., to test whether *t* is significant in a particular direction, the two-tailed *p*s at the head of the columns should be divided by 2.

level of significance with increases in the number of subjects.*

Of course, how to interpret the size of a correlation coefficient will depend on the way a researcher proposes to use it as well as on its statistical significance. A Pearson r of .40 might be satisfactorily high in the case of validity yet too low for reliability, while r = .61 would certainly be more impressive in the case of intercoder reliability. When one of two variables can be understood as an independent variable, then the binomial effect-size display (BESD) can help us to evaluate the magnitude of the effect of X on Y (discussed in Chapter 11).

COMPUTING F AND t IN RANDOMIZED DESIGNS

To illustrate the computation of the F ratio (discussed in Chapter 12) we return to the earlier example of some hypothetical effects of nutrition on the academic performance of 12 subjects. In our earlier discussion, we compared two alternative results, which we repeat in Table A.3 along with column sums and means.

The numerator of the F ratio (the mean square between conditions or the dispersion among condition means) is defined as:

$$\text{Mean square}_{\text{between}} = \frac{T_1^2/n_1 + T_2^2/n_2 + \cdots + T_a^2/n_a - (\text{Total})^2/N}{a - 1}$$

where T_1 = the sum of the scores of the first group
T_2 = the sum of the scores of the second group
T_a = the sum of the scores of the ath or last group
n_1 = the number of cases or scores of the first group
n_2 = the number of cases or scores of the second group
n_a = the number of cases or scores of the ath or last group

N = the number of cases or scores added over all groups
Total = the sum of the scores added over all groups
a = the number of groups being compared

Results A and results B in Table A.3 have identical numerators for their respective variance ratios:

*The smaller the *actual* size of the effect, obviously the more observations will be needed to detect it at a given level of significance. Suppose that a researcher hoped to detect what is *in fact* a "small" relationship between two variables (that is, r = .10) at $p < .05$. To detect such a relationship with power $(1 - \beta)$ equal to .50, it would be necessary to have nearly 400 pairs of observations (N = 384). On the other hand, to detect what is *in fact* a "medium" relationship (r = .30) at the same significance level ($p < .05$) and power $(1 - \beta = .50)$, the researcher would need only about one-tenth (N = 42) the number of observations called for previously. For further discussion of this aspect of data analysis, see Cohen (1969, 1977) or Chapter 24 in Rosenthal and Rosnow (1984).

TABLE A.3

SOME HYPOTHETICAL EFFECTS OF NUTRITION ON THE ACADEMIC
PERFORMANCE OF TWELVE SUBJECTS: ALTERNATIVE RESULTS FOR
FULLY RANDOMIZED DESIGN

	Treatment conditions			
	Group I zero	Group II milk	Group III vitamins	Group IV hot lunch
Alternative results A	$S_1 = 8$ $S_5 = 10$ $S_9 = 12$	$S_2 = 10$ $S_6 = 12$ $S_{10} = 14$	$S_3 = 13$ $S_7 = 15$ $S_{11} = 17$	$S_4 = 17$ $S_8 = 19$ $S_{12} = 21$
	Sum = 30	Sum = 36	Sum = 45	Sum = 57
	Mean = 10	Mean = 12	Mean = 15	Mean = 19
Alternative results B	$S_1 = 4$ $S_5 = 10$ $S_9 = 16$	$S_2 = 6$ $S_6 = 12$ $S_{10} = 18$	$S_3 = 9$ $S_7 = 15$ $S_{11} = 21$	$S_4 = 13$ $S_8 = 19$ $S_{12} = 25$
	Sum = 30	Sum = 36	Sum = 45	Sum = 57
	Mean = 10	Mean = 12	Mean = 15	Mean = 19

$$\frac{(30)^2/3 + (36)^2/3 + \cdots + (57)^2/3 - (168)^2/12}{4 - 1} = \frac{138}{3} = 46$$

The denominator of the F ratio (the mean square within conditions or the dispersion within conditions) is defined as:

Mean square$_{within}$ =

$$\frac{X_1^2 + X_2^2 + \cdots + X_N^2 - T_1^2/n_1 - T_2^2/n_2 - \cdots - T_a^2/n_a}{N - a}$$

where X_1 is the first individual score, X_2 the second individual score, and X_N the Nth or last individual score.

Result A, then, has the following denominator for the F ratio:

$$\frac{(8)^2 + (10)^2 + \cdots + (21)^2 - (30)^2/3 - (36)^2/3 - \cdots - (57)^2/3}{12 - 4} =$$

$$\frac{32}{8} = 4,$$

while result B of Table 6 has the denominator:

$$\frac{(4)^2 + (6)^2 + \cdots + (25)^2 - (30)^2/3 - (36)^2/3 - \cdots - (57)^2/3}{12 - 4} =$$

$$\frac{288}{8} = 36,$$

which makes the F ratio ($46/36 = 1.28$) for results B only one-ninth the size of the F ratio ($46/4 = 11.50$) for results A. Tables are available that show us for any particular F the probability (p) that an F of that size or larger might have occurred by chance (i.e., if the groups did not really differ). Reference to Table A.4, which shows a sample listing of F values corresponding to different probability levels, reveals that result A could have occurred by chance less than five times in a thousand, while result B could have occurred by chance very, very often.

To illustrate the computation of t from F, suppose that we conducted an experiment not of four groups but of only two, such that we compared one group of children given vitamins with another group of children who received nothing. Columns I and III in Table A.3 showing alternative results A and B can be used to show the relationship between F and t. In Chapter 12, we mentioned that the simplest way to think of the t statistic is that it is the square root of the appropriate F ratio computed for only two groups. As with F, the larger the t value the more unlikely

TABLE A.4
SAMPLE LISTING OF F VALUES

Groups	N-a	Probability levels			
		.10	.05	.01	.005
	4	4.54	7.71	21.20	31.33
	8	3.46	5.32	11.26	14.69
$a = 2$	16	3.05	4.49	8.53	10.58
	40	2.84	4.08	7.31	8.83
	∞	2.71	3.84	6.64	7.88
	4	4.32	6.94	18.00	26.28
	8	3.11	4.46	8.65	11.04
$a = 3$	16	2.67	3.63	6.23	7.51
	40	2.44	3.23	5.18	6.07
	∞	2.30	2.99	4.60	5.30
	4	4.19	6.59	16.69	24.26
	8	2.92	4.07	7.59	9.60
$a = 4$	16	2.46	3.24	5.29	6.30
	40	2.23	2.84	4.31	4.98
	∞	2.08	2.60	3.78	4.28

N = total number of subjects in all groups combined. $N-a$ is called the degrees of freedom (df) of the denominator of F.

a = number of groups being compared; (a-1) is called the degrees of freedom (df) of the numerator of F.

that the variation between group means represented by the t value could have arisen if the groups did not really differ. The magnitude of t increases just as F does, not only as the dispersion between means or group averages increases but also as the dispersion of scores within groups decreases.

If we follow the calculations for F given earlier for just the groups in columns I and III in Table A.3, we find $F = 9.38$ for results A and $F = 1.04$ for results B. The corresponding t values are 3.06 ($p < .05$) and 1.02 ($p > .35$), suggesting that for results A, the 5-point superiority of the vitamin group over the zero group means more than does the same degree of average difference found in results B. Note also that, for the *two-group comparison situation* in the sample listing of F values required to reach various levels of significance, these values are simply the square of the analogous t values of the sample listing of t required to reach various levels of significance.

COMPUTING F IN FACTORIAL DESIGNS

To illustrate the computation of F in a factorial design we refer again to the two-dimensional arrangement discussed in Chapter 12, the results of which are reiterated in Table A.5.

TABLE A.5
SOME HYPOTHETICAL EFFECTS OF NUTRITION ON ACADEMIC PERFORMANCE: TWO-DIMENSIONAL DESIGN

Treatment conditions	No milk	Milk	
No vitamins	$S_1 = 8$	$S_2 = 10$	
	$S_5 = 10$	$S_6 = 12$	
	$S_9 = 12$	$S_{10} = 14$	
	Sum = 30	Sum = 36	Row sum = 66
	Mean = 10	Mean = 12	Row mean = 11
Vitamins	$S_3 = 13$	$S_4 = 17$	
	$S_7 = 15$	$S_8 = 19$	
	$S_{11} = 17$	$S_{12} = 21$	
	Sum = 45	Sum = 57	Row sum = 102
	Mean = 15	Mean = 19	Row mean = 17
	Column sum = 75	Column sum = 93	Grand sum = 168
	Column mean = 12.5	Column mean = 15.5	Grand mean = 14

Table A.6 shows a typical summary of an analysis of variance, based in this case on the data in Table A.5. We find in this table two familiar entries, lines 1 and 5. Line 1 shows the variation among the four cell means that we had computed earlier. We recall the computation of line 1 as follows:

$$\frac{(30)^2/3 + (36)^2/3 + \cdots + (57)^2/3 - (168)^2/12}{4 - 1} = \frac{138}{3}$$

$$= \frac{(\text{sum of squares})}{(\text{degrees of freedom, } df)} = \text{mean square} = 46$$

Line 5 shows the variation among the individual subjects within the four conditions of the experiment with computations as follows:

$$\frac{(8)^2 + (10)^2 + \cdots + (21)^2 - (30)^2/3 - (36)^2/3 - \cdots - (57)^2/3}{12 - 4} = \frac{32}{8}$$

$$= \frac{(\text{sum of squares})}{(\text{degrees of freedom, } df)} = \text{mean square} = 4$$

The last entry of line 1 shows the ratio of the mean square between the groups to the mean square within the groups. This ratio, the F ratio, was 11.50 as we recall from our earlier example. Reference to the sample listing of F values showed us that an F of that magnitude is likely to occur very rarely unless there are real differences among the means of the four conditions.

So far we have had only a review of what was learned earlier. What we want to do now is to see the difference between the analysis of a one-dimensional design and a two-dimensional design. What we shall do is to subdivide the between-groups varia-

TABLE A. 6
ANALYSIS OF VARIANCE OF A TWO-DIMENSIONAL DESIGN

Source of variation	Sum of squares	df [a]	Mean squares	F
1 Between conditions [b]	138	$(a-1)$ = 3	46	11.50
2 Milk	27	$(c-1)$ = 1	27	6.75
3 Vitamins	108	$(r-1)$ = 1	108	27.00
4 Milk × vitamins	3	$(c-1)(r-1)$ = 1	3	0.75
5 Within conditions	32	$(N-a)$ = 8	4	—

[a] The symbols in the df column are defined as follows: a = total number of conditions; c = number of columns; r = number of rows; and N = total number of subjects.
[b] Line 1 is included only to show how lines 2, 3, and 4 are subdivisions of the total between conditions sum of squares.

tion into the three components found in lines 2, 3, and 4. These three sources of variation are referred to as (a) the main effect of milk, (b) the main effect of vitamins, and (c) the interaction effect of milk and vitamins.

The variation associated with each of these three effects can be compared to the variation within conditions so that we can compute an F ratio for each that will permit inferences about the likelihood that effects of the obtained magnitude might have occurred by chance. The denominator for all three F ratios is the same: the mean square for within conditions. The numerators for the three F ratios are as follows:

1. Mean square for main effect of milk (columns):

$$\frac{(T_{c_1})^2/n_{c_1} + (T_{c_2})^2/n_{c_2} + \cdots + (T_{c_c})^2/n_{c_c} - (\text{Total})^2/N}{a_c - 1}$$

$$= \frac{(\text{sum of squares})}{(\text{degrees of freedom, } df)} = \text{mean square}$$

where T_{c_1} = the sum of the scores of the first column
T_{c_2} = the sum of the scores of the second column
T_{c_c} = the sum of the scores of the cth or last column
n_{c_1} = the number of scores of the first column
n_{c_2} = the number of scores of the second column
n_{c_c} = the number of scores of the cth or last column
Total = the sum of the scores added over all columns
a_c = the number of columns in the experiment

2. Mean square for main effect of vitamins (rows):

$$\frac{(T_{r_1})^2/n_{r_1} + (T_{r_2})^2/n_{r_2} + \cdots + (T_{r_r})^2/n_{r_r} - (\text{Total})^2/N}{a_r - 1}$$

$$= \frac{(\text{sum of squares})}{(\text{degrees of freedom, } df)} = \text{mean square}$$

where T_{r_1} = the sum of the scores of the first row
T_{r_2} = the sum of the scores of the second row
T_{r_r} = the sum of the scores of the rth or last row
n_{r_1} = the number of scores of the first row
n_{r_2} = the number of scores of the second row
n_{r_r} = the number of scores of the rth or last row
Total = the sum of the scores added over all rows
a_r = the number of rows in the experiment

3. Mean square for interaction of rows and columns:

$$\frac{(T_1^2/n_1 + T_2^2/n_2 + \cdots + T_a^2/n_a - (\text{Total})^2/N - \begin{matrix}(\text{sum of} \\ \text{squares} \\ \text{for rows})\end{matrix} - \begin{matrix}(\text{sum of} \\ \text{squares for} \\ \text{columns})\end{matrix}}{(a_c - 1)(a_r - 1)}$$

where T_1 = the sum of the scores of the first group or cell
   T_2 = the sum of the scores of the second group or cell
   T_a = the sum of the scores of the ath or last group or cell
   n_1 = the number of scores of the first group or cell
   n_2 = the number of scores of the second group or cell
   n_a = the number of scores of the ath or last group or cell
   N = the number of scores added over all groups or cells
   Total = the sum of the scores added over all groups or cells
   a = the number of groups or cells = $(a_c \times a_r)$

(A restriction on the computational formula given for the two-dimensional design is that the number of scores in each of the cells or conditions must be proportional from column to column and from row to row.)

For these two-dimensional data, the mean square for the effect of milk is:

$$\frac{(75)^2/6 + (93)^2/6 - (168)^2/12}{2 - 1} = \frac{27}{1} = 27$$

The main effect of vitamins has an associated mean square of:

$$\frac{(66)^2/6 + (102)^2/6 - (168)^2/12}{2 - 1} = \frac{108}{1} = 108$$

The interaction mean square is:

$$\frac{(30)^2/3 + (36)^2/3 + \cdots + (57)^2/3 - (168)^2/12 - 27 - 108}{(2 - 1)(2 - 1)} = \frac{3}{1} = 3$$

The mean squares computed above are found in the analysis of variance summary table along with the F ratios formed by dividing each by the mean square for within conditions (Table A.6). Reference to the sample listing of F values in Table A.4 (for $a = 2$, since only two conditions are being compared at a time) tells us that the F of 6.75 for the effect of milk could have occurred by chance less than five times in a hundred ($p < .05$). The F of 27.00 for the effect of vitamins could have occurred by chance even less often ($p < .005$). The F for interaction, however, is so small that it could easily have arisen by chance. What we have learned from the subdivision of the between groups variation into the three components is that both milk and vitamins have a beneficial effect with more of the effect attributable to vitamins than to milk.

REPEATED-MEASURES DESIGNS

This third basic design, also referred to as a *treatments-by-subjects design,* can be seen as a special case of a two-dimensional design as noted in Chapter 12. One dimension is the main effect of the treatments while the other dimension is the array of subjects. Because there is only a single score for each subject entered for each condition, there can be no estimate of within condition variation, but an F test of the main effect of treatments is often still possible. In this case, the mean square for treatments is divided by the mean square for the treatments-times-subjects interaction.

Table A.7 illustrates this design for our four familiar treatment conditions, each of which has been applied successively to each of three different subjects. Also shown is the analysis of variance computed on these data. Since our aim here is only to be illustrative, we do not present the computational formulas required;

TABLE A.7

SOME HYPOTHETICAL EFFECTS OF NUTRITION ON PERFORMANCE: TREATMENTS-BY-SUBJECTS DESIGN

	Treatment conditions				
	Cond. I zero	Cond. II milk	Cond. III vitamins	Cond. IV hot lunch	Totals
Subject 1	8	12	15	21	56
Subject 2	10	14	17	19	60
Subject 3	12	10	13	17	52
Sums	30	36	45	57	168
Means	10	12	15	19	14

Source	Sum of squares	df	Mean squares	F
Treatments	138	3	46	11.50
Subjects	8	2	4	—
Treatments × subjects	24	6	4	—

however, they follow precisely the logic of the computational formulas presented in the preceding section.

CHI-SQUARE

In our discussion of the correlation coefficient (r), we noted that it could be viewed quite directly as a measure of the degree of relationship between two variables. Indeed, we had only to square r to obtain the proportion of variance of one of the variables estimable from a knowledge of the other variable. However, when the number of pairs of scores on which r is based is small, a very large r may not differ significantly from chance. In that case, we would be forced to say that although there was a strong relationship between our two variables, relationships that strong could occur quite often by chance even if the true correlation between our variables were zero. For that reason we would like to know for any r not only its size but also its probability of having occurred by chance. We therefore gave a formula for testing this probability by means of a t test.

While r tells us immediately how "big" a relationship there is between variables but not how unlikely it is to have occurred by chance, F and t tell us immediately how unlikely it is that a given relationship could have occurred by chance but not how "big" the relationship is. However, by taking a simple additional step, described earlier, we can compute the size of the relationship that a large F or t has convinced us is unlikely to have occurred by chance. Thus, r gives us size of relationship and permits us further to assess statistical significance, while F and t give us statistical significance and permit us further to assess the size of relationship.

The statistic we discuss in this section is the chi-square, symbolized as χ^2. It is a statistic that, like F and t, tells us how unlikely it is that the relationship investigated could have occurred by chance, but like F and t, does not tell us immediately about the strength of the relationship between the variables. Just as in the case of F and t, any given value of χ^2 will be associated with a stronger degree of relationship when it is based on a smaller number of subjects. To put it another way, a relationship must be quite strong to result in a large χ^2 (or F, or t) with only a small number of subjects.

Chi-square does its job of testing the relationship between variables by assessing the discrepancy between a theoretically expected and an obtained frequency. It differs from the other tests of association we have examined in that it can be used for dependent variables that are not scored or scaled. In all the earlier examples, subjects' responses were recorded as scores such that some could be regarded as so many units greater or less than other scores. The χ^2 statistic allows us to deal with categories of response that are not so easily ordered, scaled, or scored, as illustrated in Table A.8.

Suppose, for example, that we wanted to learn whether there was any association between subjects' membership in one of several political parties and their preference for any one of several alternative candidates for political office. Membership in a political party is thought of as the independent variable, while the preference for Smith, Brown, or Jones is the dependent variable as shown in the top section. Each member of the sample of subjects asked to state their preference falls into one and only one of the nine possible cells. The frequencies in the cell refer to the number of people in that column (party) who prefer the particular candidate listed in that row. Thus, there are 14 members of the sample who affiliated with Party II and who prefer candidate Smith, while 11 members of Party I prefer Brown, etc.

In order to compute χ^2, we must first determine for each cell of Table A.8 the number of expected entries. This expected fre-

TABLE A.8
SOME HYPOTHETICAL PARTY MEMBERSHIPS AND PREFERENCES FOR POLITICAL CANDIDATES: CHI-SQUARE

	Candidates	Party I	Party II	Party III	Row totals
Obtained	Smith	15	14	7	36
frequences (O)	Jones	14	3	10	27
	Brown	11	13	3	27
	Column totals	40	30	20	90
Expected	Smith	16	12	8	36
frequencies (E)	Jones	12	9	6	27
	Brown	12	9	6	27
	Column totals	40	30	20	90
$\dfrac{(O - E)^2}{E}$	Smith	.06	.33	.12	.51
	Jones	.33	4.00	2.67	7.00
	Brown	.08	1.78	1.50	3.36
	Column totals	.47	6.11	4.29	10.87

$$\chi^2 = \sum \frac{(O - E)^2}{E} = .06 + .33 + .12 \cdots + 1.78 + 1.50 = 10.87.$$

quency is computed for each cell by multiplying the column total by the row total for that row and that column that intersect in the cell in question, then dividing this quantity by the grand total number of entries. The upper left cell of the top section is at the intersection of column I and Smith's row. The appropriate totals multiplied together and divided by the grand total are thus: (Column total $\times$ Row total)/Total $N = (40)(36)/90 = 16$. The expected frequency for the cell formed at the intersection of column III and Brown's row is: $(20)(27)/90 = 6$. The second section gives all the expected frequencies computed in this way. The third section gives for each cell the square of the difference between the obtained and expected frequency divided by the expected frequency. For just the first row, these values are: $(15-16)^2/16$, $(14-12)^2/12$, $(7-8)^2/8 = .06, .33$, and $.12$. The total of all these values is the χ^2, which in this case is 10.87.

The larger the χ^2, the less likely it is that the obtained frequencies differ only by chance from the expected frequencies. Shown in Table A.9 is a sample listing of χ^2 values for each of a number of p values. To find the appropriate line on which to enter the table, we multiply the number of rows less one $(3 - 1)$ times the number of columns less one $(3 - 1)$ to obtain the value 4. The number obtained by multiplying (number of rows minus one, or $R - 1$) by (number of columns minus one, or $C - 1$) is called the degrees of freedom (df) of the chi-square. Our obtained value of χ^2 was 10.87, which falls between the .05 and .01 levels of statistical significance. There are, then, less than five chances in a hundred that a χ^2 so large could have occurred if there were really no relationship between party membership and preferred candidate.

TABLE A.9
SAMPLE LISTING OF χ^2 VALUES

	Probability levels			
(R–1) (C–1)	**.10**	**.05**	**.01**	**.005**
1	2.71	3.84	6.63	7.88
2	4.61	5.99	9.21	10.60
4	7.78	9.49	13.28	14.86
8	13.36	15.51	20.09	21.96
24	33.20	36.42	42.98	45.56

R = number of rows.
C = number of columns.
$(R–1)$ $(C–1)$ is called the degrees of freedom (df) of the chi-square.

When there are many cells in a χ^2 table, a statisticaly significant χ^2 may be difficult to interpret. The construction of an intermediate table such as that of the bottom section can be of help. The entries of that section show which of the cells contributed most to the overall large χ^2. A large cell entry in this table of $(O - E)^2/E$ values indicates that the cell in question is surprising to us, or unexpected, given the magnitude of the row and column totals that are affected by that cell. The largest value of this section suggests that for Party II, surprisingly few members voted for Jones; the second largest value suggests that for Party III, surprisingly many members voted for Jones.

REPORTING EFFECT SIZES

In contemporary data analytic work, it is becoming increasingly important that every time researchers report a test of significance they also report the corresponding magnitude of the effect. Although there are many different estimates of effect size, we discuss just one in this section—the Pearson r. It is widely used and, especially when employed in the context of the BESD (see Chapter 11), it is easy to interpret in terms of the practical importance of the size of the obtained effect.

When our test of significance is t, we find the corresponding effect size r from the following:

$$r = \sqrt{\frac{t^2}{t^2 + df}}$$

When our test of significance is F and the numerator of the F test has only one df, we can find the corresponding effect size r from the following:

$$r = \sqrt{\frac{F}{F + df \text{ error}}}$$

When our test of significance is χ^2 and when $df = 1$, i.e., $(R-1)(C-1) = 1$, we can find the corresponding effect size r from the following:

$$r = \sqrt{\frac{\chi^2}{N}}$$

The use of effect size estimates based on F with more than 1 df in the numerator or based on χ^2 with more than 1 df is problematic. Such effect size estimates are difficult to interpret properly and are less useful than is commonly realized. For these reasons we do not discuss them here. They are discussed in Rosenthal and Rosnow (1984).

GLOSSARY

abscissa The horizontal axis of a distribution; the X-axis.

alpha (α) Probability of a type I error; the significance, or p, level.

analysis of variance Subdivision of the total variance of a set of scores into its components.

area probability sampling A type of probability sampling where the subclasses are geographical areas.

arithmetic mean Arithmetic average, that is, $\overline{X} = \Sigma X/N$.

artifacts Specific threats to validity (internal, external, construct), or confounded aspects of the scientist's observations.

assumed probability A probability that is taken for granted, where there is scientific evidence for belief that a particular relationship or phenomenon is likely to occur or prove true.

average deviation The average distance from the mean of all scores.

BESD See *binomial effect size display*.

beta (β) Probability of a type II error.

bimodal A distribution showing two modes.

binomial effect size display (BESD) Procedure for the display of the practical importance of a correlation (r) of any particular magnitude where one variable is understood to be the independent variable.

biosocial experimenter effects Those interactional artifacts that are a function of biosocial attributes of the experimenter.

blind controls Research participants who are unaware of their experimental status.

causal inference The act or process of inferring that X causes Y.

central tendency Location of the bulk of a distribution measured by means, medians, modes, trimmed means, etc.

chi-square (χ^2)   A statistical employed with frequency data to test the degree of agreement between the data actually obtained and those expected under a particular hypothesis (e.g., the null hypothesis).

closed method   A method that is anchored in experiences that set a decisive limit to its field of application.

coefficient of correlation   Index of correlation, typically Pearson r, or related product-moment correlation.

concept   Thought, idea, cognition.

concurrent validity   A type of test validity that asks the extent to which the test results are correlated with some criterion in the present.

confounded variables   Uncontrolled variables that are correlated with one another.

construct   An abstract variable that is constructed from hypothetical ideas or images in order to serve as an explanatory term.

construct validation   The strategy by which a means for the measurement of a construct is devised and then related to subjects' performance in a variety of other spheres as the construct would predict. *Construct validity* is concerned with the psychological qualities contributing to the relationship between X and Y.

contextualist paradigm   The global view that human behavior can be best understood only as part of a total context of events.

control group   A condition against which researchers compare the effects of the treatment (or experimental) condition. Also, a procedure to serve as a check on validity.

correlated replicators   Observers or researchers who are not independent of one another.

correlation   Degree of relationship between variables.

covary   That variations in one variable are correlated with variations in another.

criterion variable   An outcome variable, a variable that was predicted.

cross-lag design   A diachronic research design where one variable is allowed to lag behind the other, thus using relational data to test a causal hypothesis.

crude range   Highest score minus lowest score.

D The difference between scores or ranks.

$\overline{D}$ The mean of a set of Ds.

degrees of freedom   The number of observations minus the number of restrictions limiting the observations' freedom to vary.

demand characteristics   The mixture of various inadvertent hints and cues that govern the subject's perception of his or her role and of the experimenter's hypothesis.

dependent variable   A variable whose changes are viewed as being dependent or consequent on changes in one or more independent variables.

descriptive inquiry   Any method of research that seeks to map out what happens behaviorally, to tell "how things are."

determinative relationship   The assumption that changes in one variable probably serve to determine changes in another variable.

df Degrees of freedom.

diachronic research Referring to a temporal research approach in which a phenomenon or variable is observed in such a way as to uncover changes that occur during successive periods of time (e.g., longitudinal research).

difference in success rates See *binomial effect size display*.

disguised instruments Those measuring instruments that are used to study behavior indirectly or unobtrusively.

dispersion Spread or variability.

distribution The relative frequencies as we move over varying values of the independent variable.

drunkard's search The principle that much effort is lost or vitiated when researchers look in a convenient place but not in the most likely one.

effect size The magnitude of an experimental effect; the degree to which the relationship studied differs from zero.

empirical method Any effective manner or mode of procedure using experience, observation, or experiment to map out the nature of reality.

equivalent-forms method A means of evaluating reliability in test construction based on data from comparable forms of the same test.

error term The denominator of an F ratio in the analysis of variance.

errors Deviations of scores from the mean of the group or condition.

ethics The system of moral values by which behavior is judged.

evaluation apprehension The anxiety state in which subjects experience apprehension that an experimenter intends to evaluate some aspect of their competence, for example, how bright they are, whether they are well adjusted, or some other facet of their personalities.

expectancy control design A research design in which the expectancy variable is designed to operate independently from the primary independent variable.

expected frequencies Counts expected under various conditions if certain hypotheses (e.g., the null hypothesis) were true.

experimental group A group in which there is controlled manipulation of some independent variable.

experimental inquiry Any method of research that seeks to describe what happens behaviorally when something of interest to the experimenter is introduced into the situation, to tell "how things are and how they got to be that way."

experimenter One who tests or tries some observational method, using human or animal subjects, in order to gather scientific data about behavior.

experimenter expectancy effect That artifact that results when the hypothesis held by the investigator leads unintentionally to behavior toward subjects that increases the likelihood that their behavior, in turn, will confirm the hypothesis.

extended range Crude range plus one unit.

external validity The approximate validity with which conclusions are drawn about the generalizability of a relationship.

external variables Independent variables that can "pull" a human being in a particular direction or toward a specific goal or object.

F **ratios** Ratios of mean squares that are distributed as *F* when the null hypothesis is true.

F **test** A test of significance employed to judge the tenability of the null hypothesis of no relationship between two or more variables.

factorial designs Experimental designs in which each level of one dimension or factor is administered in combination with each level of another dimension or factor.

false precision When something relatively vague is reported as if the measuring instrument were sensitive to very slight differences.

falsifiability The principle that a theoretical system is "scientific" only if it is stated in such a way that it can, if incorrect, be falsified by empirical tests.

field experiment An experiment done in a natural setting, that is, outside the laboratory.

forced-choice Where the respondent is "forced" to accept some statements that are clearly unfavorable or to reject some statements that are clearly favorable.

frequency distribution. A set of data scores arranged according to incidence of occurrence.

fully randomized designs Designs in which there are two or more groups to be compared on the dependent variable and the subjects are assigned to their particular group at random.

good subject The research participant who "puts his best foot forward," by eagerly cooperating with the experimenter—a characteristic that is more common among volunteer than nonvolunteer subjects.

grand mean Mean of means.

halo effect A type of response set in which the bias results from the judge's forming a favorable impression of someone with regard to some central trait and then tending to paint a rosier picture of the person on other characteristics.

heterogeneous That certain elements are essentially different from one another.

high antecedent probability That a research idea is believed, even before being empirically tested, to be sound and likely to prove relevant to the problem under investigation.

homogeneous That certain elements are essentially alike.

hypothesis A research idea that serves as a premise or proposition to organize certain facts; a testable proposition.

hypothetical construct A conceptual variable (e.g., a prejudiced attitude) that is used to explain the occurrence of an event or particular behavior (e.g., discriminatory behavior).

independent variable A variable on which the dependent variable depends. Also, an observable or measurable event manipulated by an experimenter to determine whether there is any effect upon another event (the dependent variable).

indirect measures   Measures taken by instruments that are used to study behavior when the subject is aware of being observed but not of the consequences of his or her behavior, for example, the Rorschach test.

intentional effect   That type of noninteractional experimenter effect that results in error due to the researcher's dishonesty in reporting data.

interaction effects   Condition means minus grand mean, row effects, and column effects.

interactional experimenter effects   Those that operate by affecting the actual response of the participant.

interdisciplinary research   Research in which a scientist draws heavily on the theoretical orientations and methods of more than one field.

internal validity   The degree of validity of statements made about whether X causes Y by ruling out plausible rival hypotheses.

internal variables   Independent variables that can "push" a human being in a particular direction or toward a specific goal or object; motivational variables.

joint method   J. S. Mill's joint method of agreement and difference, which tells us whether X is both necessary and sufficient for the occurrence of Y.

learning   A relatively stable or permanent change in behavior potential that occurs as a result of practice.

linear relationship   Straight-line relationship between two or more variables.

location measures   Measures of central tendency.

mean   The arithmetic average of a set of scores.

mechanistic paradigm   The global view that compares social causation to a complex machine and assumes human nature to be a matter of social engineering.

median   The midmost score of a distribution.

metaphor   A word or phrase applied to a concept or phenomenon that it does not literally denote.

method of agreement   If X, then Y—which means that X is a sufficient condition of Y.

method of difference   If not-X, then not-Y—which means that X is a necessary condition of Y.

methodological behaviorism   The view that asserts that only empirically accessible or observable variables or relationships are suitable for scientific study.

methodological pluralism   The view that asserts that behavior is best studied by using many different kinds of empirical and conceptual strategies.

mode   The score occurring with greatest frequency.

moral neutrality   The assumption that science is value-free.

MS   Mean square.

MS **between**   Mean square between conditions.

MS **error**   Mean square used as denominator of F ratio.

MS **within**   Mean square within conditions.

N   The number of scores in a study.

n   Number of scores in a sample or subsample.

naturalistic observation   Any research that examines behavior in its usual natural environment.

necessary condition   A requisite or essential condition.

negativistic subject   The type of research participant who approaches the investigation with an uncooperative attitude.

no show   A person who volunteers to serve as a research subject, but then fails to show up; also called a *pseudovolunteer.*

nonreactive observation   Any observation that does not affect the thing being observed.

nonresponse bias   Error that is due to nonresponse or nonparticipation.

normal distribution   Bell-shaped curve that is completely described by mean and standard deviation.

null hypothesis   The hypothesis that there is no relationship between two or more variables.

numerical scale   A rating scale in which the judges work with a sequence of defined numbers.

observed frequencies   Counts obtained under various conditions.

observer effect   That type of noninteractional experimenter effect that results in overstatements or understatements of some criterion value during the observation and recording phase of the research process.

Occam's razor   The principle that hypotheses introduced to explain relationships should be as economical or parsimonious as possible. Also known as the *principle of parsimony.*

open-ended item   See *unstructured items.*

operational definition   The meaning of a variable in terms of the operations necessary to measure it in any concrete situation, or in terms of the experimental methods involved in its determination.

ordinate   The vertical axis of a distribution; the Y-axis.

p **value**   Probability value or level obtained in a test of significance.

paradigm   A conceptual view larger than a theory; a "world view."

paradigm case   A clear and exemplary model of something.

paradox of sampling   The appropriateness of a sample is validated by the method used to arrive at it.

participant observation   A method of observation in which a group or a community is studied from within by a researcher who makes careful records of the behavior as it proceeds.

Pearson *r*   Standard index of linear relationship.

pilot work   Exploratory work, or work carried out on a small scale prior to a more extensive investigation.

placebo-control group   A control group in which a substance without any pharmacological effect is given as a "drug."

plausible rival hypothesis   A proposition, or set of propositions, that provides a reasonable alternative to the working hypothesis as an explanation for the occurrence of some specified phenomenon.

pluralism   The idea that there is more than one way to do something, or more than one regulative principle (such as the mechanistic view of causality) for concretizing or objectifying perceptions of reality.

pointless precision When a measure is more exact than can be taken advantage of in the situation.

population The organisms or other units from which we have drawn our samples and to which we want to generalize.

postdictive validity A type of test validity based on the extent to which the test results correlate with some criterion in the past.

power Probability of not making a type II error, or $1 - \beta$.

precision The exactness of observations made.

predictive validity A type of test validity based on the extent to which the test can "predict" the future.

principle of parsimony See *Occam's razor*.

probability The mathematical chance of an event occurring.

probability sampling A sampling plan that specifies that the population will be divided into subclasses and then sampled in a way so as to ensure that each subclass is represented in proportion to its contribution to the population.

product-moment correlation Standard index of linear relationship.

projective tests Indirect disguised measures that operate on the principle that the subject will project some unconscious aspect of his or her life experience and emotions onto ambiguous stimuli in the spontaneous responses that come to mind, for example, the Rorschach test.

pseudosubject A confederate of the researcher.

quasi-control subjects Participants who reflect on the context in which an experiment is conducted and speculate on ways in which the context might influence their own and research subjects' behavior.

quasi-experiment Any design that resembles an experimental design (in that there are treatments, outcome measures, and experimental units) but where there is no random assignment to create the comparisons from which treatment-caused changes are inferred.

r Pearson's product-moment correlation.

r^2 Pearson's correlation squared; proportion of variance "accounted for."

random sample A sample chosen by chance procedures and with known probabilities of selection, so that every individual in the population will have the same likelihood of being selected.

range Distance between the highest and lowest score.

rating scale The common name for a variety of measuring instruments where the observer gives a numerical value to certain judgments or assessments.

reactive observation An observation that affects the thing being observed.

regulative principle A proposition whose falsity cannot be empirically demonstrated, but which influences our thinking about empirical relationships.

relational inquiry Any method of research that seeks to describe how what happens behaviorally changes along with changes in some other set of observations, to tell "how things are in relation to other things."

reliability The degree to which observations are consistent or stable.

repeated measurements Measurements made on the same sampling units.

repeated-measures designs Designs in which a number of experimental (or control) conditions are applied to each of a number of subjects.

replicability The ability to repeat or duplicate a scientific observation, often an experimental observation.

response The consequence of, or reaction to, a stimulus.

response set That type of response bias in which a person's answers to questions or responses to a set of items are determined by a consistent mental set.

response variable Dependent variable.

sample The subset of the population for whom we have obtained observations.

sampling plan A design, scheme of action, or procedure that specifies how the research participants are to be selected.

sampling units The organisms or objects being studied, e.g., people, schools, or countries.

sampling with replacement A type of simple random selection in which the selected names are placed in the selection pool again and may be reselected on subsequent draws. This is contrasted with *sampling without replacement*, in which a previously selected name cannot be reselected and must be disregarded on any later draw.

scientific method A methodical system of scientific procedures and techniques that is believed to "work" or "produce" or "pay off."

self-fulfilling prophecy The idea that someone who predicts an event may behave in ways that are likely to increase the probability that the event will occur—the prophet thus acts to fulfill his or her own prophecy.

self-selection of subjects When research participants are allowed to place themselves into or choose or assign themselves to a particular treatment group.

serendipity The occurrence of discoveries in the course of investigations designed for another purpose.

Σ Instruction telling us to sum or add a set of numbers.

σ The standard deviation of a set of scores.

σ^2 The variance of a set of scores.

significance level The level of alpha.

significance test Statistical test giving information on the tenability of the null hypothesis of no relationship between two or more variables.

significance testing The use of statistical probability when a decision is made about a hypothesis.

simple randomized design A research design in which there are two groups to be compared on the dependent variable and the subjects are placed in the groups at random so that no sampling bias can enter into their assignment to the experimental or control condition.

simple random selection   A type of sampling plan in which the participants are selected individually on the basis of a table of random digits.

small-N research   Research that uses a case study approach or, as in animal conditioning experiments, uses highly inbred animals (rats, mice, etc.) to rule out or minimize genetic differences (also called "single case research").

Solomon design   A four-group experimental design that was developed by R. L. Solomon. It is a means of assessing initial performance without having contaminated it by pretesting; it also allows us to determine the interaction of pretesting and treatment.

split-half method   A means of evaluating reliability in test construction, in which the responses to a test that is split in half are correlated.

spread   Disperson or variability.

standard deviation   An index of the variability of a set of data around the most typical value in a distribution.

standard normal curve   Normal curve with mean = 0 and $\sigma = 1$.

standard score   Score converted to standard deviation unit.

standardized measure   The fact that standards have been established for administering, scoring, and interpreting a particular measure or instrument.

statistical conclusion validity   The degree to which the presumed independent variable, X, and the presumed dependent variable, Y, are indeed related.

statistical significance   The p value selected to define the test statistic (e.g., t, F, χ^2) as too large to make the null hypothesis tenable.

stimulus   Any sensory contact that evokes a response.

strong inference   A type of research approach in which one hypothesis or fact vies against another.

structured items   Those with clearcut response options.

sufficient condition   An adequate condition.

SS   Sum of squares.

SS **between**   Sum of squares between conditions.

SS **total**   Total sum of squares.

SS **within**   Sum of squares within conditions.

symmetry   A characteristic of distributions in which the portions to the right and left of the mean are mirror images of each other.

synchronic research   A temporal approach in which a variable is observed as it exists at one brief period in time, not using information about its development; e.g., the typical lab experiment in behavioral science.

t **test**   A test of significance employed to judge the tenability of the null hypothesis of no relationship between two variables.

table analysis   Statistical analysis of frequency counts cast into tabular form.

tacit knowledge   Facts or truths that we know but cannot easily communicate verbally.

test of significance   Statistical test giving information on the tenability of the null hypothesis of no relationship between two or more variables.

test-retest method   A means of evaluating reliability in test construction in which the correlation coefficient is calculated on data obtained from the same test but from results gotten at different times.

theoretical definition   The meaning of a variable in relatively abstract terms. Also called the *conceptual definition* of a variable.

theory   A statement or series of statements consisting of generalizable propositions or hypotheses that are interrelated in order to bring order and meaning to something.

trimmed mean   The mean of a distribution from which a percentage of the highest and lowest Xs have been dropped.

type I error   The error in rejecting the null hypothesis when it is true.

type II error   The error in failing to reject the null hypothesis when it is false.

unbiased sample   A sample whose values do not differ from the corresponding values in the population being studied.

unobtrusive measures   Measures taken by instruments that are used to study behavior when the subject is unaware of being scientifically observed.

unstructured items   Those that offer the respondent an opportunity to express feelings, motives, or behavior quite spontaneously—also called *open-ended* items.

validity   The degree to which we observe what we purport to observe.

values   The standards or principles by which the worth of something is judged.

variable s   Any observable or measurable attribute that can take on two or more values.

variance   The mean of the squared deviations of scores from their mean.

volunteer bias   The error that results when participants who volunteer respond differently than nonvolunteers.

working hypothesis   A proposition, or set of propositions, that serves to guide and organize an empirical investigation.

X Any score.

$\bar{X}$ The mean of a set of scores.

X-axis   The horizontal axis of a distribution.

Y-axis   The vertical axis of a distribution.

yea-saying   A type of response set in which the person tends to answer consistently in the affirmative.

Z score   Score converted to standard deviation unit.

REFERENCES

Adorno, T. W., E. Frenkel-Brunswik, D. J. Levinson, and R. N. Sanford: *The Authoritarian Personality,* Harper & Row, New York, 1950.

Apel, K.: History of science and the problem of historical understanding and explanation, Paper presented at Conference on the Philosophy of the Human Studies, Bryn Mawr College and Temple University, October 17, 1981.

————: C. S. Peirce and the post-Tarskian problem of an adequate explication of the meaning of truth: Towards a transcendental-pragmatic theory of truth, part II, *Transactions of the Charles S. Peirce Society,* 1982, *18,* 3–17.

Arellano-Galdames, F. J.: Some ethical problems in research on human subjects, unpublished doctoral dissertation, University of New Mexico, 1972.

Asch, S.: *Social Psychology,* Prentice-Hall, Englewood Cliffs, N.J., 1952.

Atwell, J. E.: Human rights in human subjects research, in A. J. Kimmel (ed.), *New Directions for Methodology of Social and Behavioral Science: Ethics of Human Subject Research,* no. 10, Jossey-Bass, San Francisco, 1981, pp. 81–90.

Axinn, S.: Fallacy of the single risk, *Philosophy of Science,* 1966, *33,* 154–162.

Boring, E. G.: *A History of Experimental Psychology* (2d ed.), Appleton-Century-Crofts, New York, 1950.

Brady, J. V.: Ulcers in "executive" monkeys, *Scientific American,* 1958, *199,* 95–100.

———, R. W. Porter, D. G. Conrad, and J. W. Mason: Avoidance behavior and the development of gastroduodenal ulcers, *Journal for the Experimental Analysis of Behavior,* 1958, *1,* 69–72.

Bridgman, P. W.: *The Logic of Modern Physics,* Macmillan, New York, 1937.

Brogden, W. J.: Animal studies of learning, in S. S. Stevens (ed.), *Handbook of Experimental Psychology,* Wiley, New York, 1951, pp. 568–612.

Buranelli, V.: *The Wizard from Vienna: Franz Anton Mesmer,* Coward, McCann & Geoghegan, New York, 1975.

Campbell, D. T., and J. C. Stanley: *Experimental and Quasi-Experimental Designs for Research,* Rand McNally, Chicago, 1966.

Cannon, W. B.: *The Way of an Investigator,* Norton, New York, 1945.

Caws, P.: *The Philosophy of Science: A Systematic Account,* Van Nostrand, Princeton, 1965.

Chamberlin, T. C.: The method of multiple working hypotheses, *Journal of Geology,* 1897, *5,* 838–848.

Christensen, H. T.: Cultural relativism and premarital sex norms, *American Sociological Review,* 1960, *25,* 31–39.

Cohen, J.: *Statistical Power Analysis for the Behavioral Sciences,* Academic Press, New York, 1969 (rev. ed., 1977).

Cohen, M. R.: *Reason and Nature: An Essay on the Meaning of Scientific Method,* Dover, New York, 1959 (first published 1931, Harcourt Brace).

Collins, H. M.: Science and the rule of replicability: A sociological study of scientific method, Paper presented at annual meeting of the American Association for the Advancement of Science in symposium on "Replication and Experimenter Effect," Washington, D.C., 1978.

Columbo, J.: The critical period concept: Research, methodology, and theoretical issues, *Psychological Bulletin,* 1982, *91,* 260–275.

Converse, J.: Issue-importance and forced-compliance attitude change: Another curvilinear finding, *Personality and Social Psychology Bulletin,* 1982, *8,* 651–655.

Cook, T. D., and D. T. Campbell: *Quasi-Experimentation: Design and Analysis Issues for Field Settings,* Rand McNally, Chicago, 1979.

Cooper, J., L. Eisenberg, J. Robert, and B. S. Dohrenwend: The effect of experimenter expectancy and preparatory effort on belief in the probable occurrence of future events, *Journal of Social Psychology,* 1967, *71,* 221–226.

Couch, A., and K. Keniston: Yeasayers and naysayers: Agreeing response set as a personality variable, *Journal of Abnormal and Social Psychology,* 1960, *60,* 151–174.

Cronbach, L. J., and P. E. Meehl: Construct validity in psychological tests, *Psychological Bulletin,* 1955, *52,* 281–302.

Crowne, D. P., and D. Marlowe: *The Approval Motive: Studies in Evaluative Dependence,* Wiley, New York, 1964.

Dohrenwend, B. S.: Interviewer biasing effects: Toward a reconciliation of findings, *Public Opinion Quarterly,* 1969, *33,* 121–125.

————, J. Colombotos, and B. P. Dohrenwend: Social distance and interviewer effects, *Public Opinion Quarterly*, 1968, *32*, 410–422.

Dollard, J., L. W. Doob, N. E. Miller, O. H. Mowrer, R. R. Sears, (C. S. Ford, C. I. Hovland, and R. T. Sollenberger): *Frustration and Aggression*, Yale University Press, New Haven, 1939.

Duhem, P.: *The Aim and Structure of Physical Theory*, Princeton University Press, Princeton, 1954.

Eagly, A. H.: Sex differences in influenceability, *Psychological Bulletin*, 1978, *85*, 86–116.

Easley, J. A.: Scientific method as an educational objective, in L. C. Deighton (Ed.), *The Encyclopedia of Education*, Free Press and Macmillan, New York, 1971, vol. 8, pp. 150–157.

Eron, L. D., and L. R. Huesmann: Sohn should let sleeping dogs lie, *American Psychologist*, 1980, *36*, 231–233.

————, ————, M. M. Lefkowitz, and L. O. Walder: Does television violence cause aggression? *American Psychologist*, 1972, *27*, 253–263.

Esposito, J. L., and R. L. Rosnow: Corporate rumors: How they start and how to stop them, *Management Review*, 1983, *72*, No. 4, 44–49.

Feldman, R. E.: Response to compatriot and foreigner who seek assistance, *Journal of Personality and Social Psychology*, 1968, *10*, 202–214.

Festinger, L.: *A Theory of Cognitive Dissonance*, Row, Peterson, Evanston, Ill., 1957.

Fisher, R. A.: *The Design of Experiments*, Oliver & Boyd, London, 1935.

Gallup, G.: Lessons learned in 40 years of polling, Paper presented before National Council on Public Polls, May 21, 1976.

Gergen, K. J.: Social psychology as history, *Journal of Personality and Social Psychology*, 1973, *26*, 309–320.

Greenwald, A. G., and D. L. Ronis: Twenty years of cognitive dissonance: Case study of the evolution of a theory, *Psychological Review*, 1978, *85*, 53–57.

Grünbaum, A.: Causality and the science of human behavior, *American Scientist*, 1952, *40*, 665–676.

Grusky, O.: The effects of formal structure on managerial recruitment: A study of baseball organization, *Sociometry*, 1963, *26*, 345–353. (a)

————: Managerial succession and organizational effectiveness, *American Journal of Sociology*, 1963, *69*, 21–31. (b)

Harlow, H. F.: Love in infant monkeys, in S. Coopersmith (ed.), *Frontiers of Psychological Research*, W. H. Freeman, San Francisco, 1959, 1966.

————, and M. K. Harlow: The affectional system, in A. M. Schrier, H. F. Harlow, and F. Stollnitz (eds.), *Behavior of Nonhuman Primates: Modern Research Trends*, vol. 2, Academic Press, New York, 1965, pp. 287–334.

————, and ————: Learning to love, *American Scientist*, 1966, *54*, 244–272.

————, and ————: The young monkeys, in P. Cramer (ed.), *Readings in Developmental Psychology*, CRM Books, Del Mar, Calif., 1970, pp. 93–97.

Henry, W. E.: *The Analysis of Fantasy*, Wiley, New York, 1956.

Hilgard, E. R.: Introduction, in G. J. Bloch (ed.), *Mesmerism: A Translation of the Original Medical and Scientific Writings of F. A. Mesmer, M. D.*, William Kaufmann, Los Altos, Calif., 1980.

Jones, F. P.: Experimental method in antiquity, *American Psychologist*, 1964, *19*, 419.

Kamin, L.: *The Science and Politics of IQ*, Erlbaum, Potomac, Md., 1974.

Kaplan, A.: *The Conduct of Inquiry: Methodology for Behavioral Science*, Chandler, Scranton, Pa., 1964.

Katona, G.: *Psychological Economics*, Elsevier, New York, 1975.

————: Toward a macropsychology, *American Psychologist*, 1979, *34*, 118–126.

Kazdin, A. E., and A. H. Tuma (eds.): New Directions for Methodology of Social and Behavioral Research: Single-Case Research Designs, no.13, Jossey-Bass, San Francisco, 1982.

Kendler, H. H.: The reality of operationism, *Journal of Mind and Behavior*, 1981, *2*, 331–341.

Kenny, D. A.: *Correlation and Causality*, Wiley, New York, 1979.

Kinsey, A. C., W. B. Pomeroy, C. E. Martin, and P. H. Gebhard: *Sexual Behavior in the Human Female*, Saunders, Philadelphia, 1953.

Kuhn, T. S.: *The Structure of Scientific Revolutions*, University of Chicago Press, Chicago, 1962.

Lana, R. E.: *Assumptions of Social Psychology*, Appleton-Century-Crofts, New York, 1969..

————, and R. L. Rosnow: *Introduction to Contemporary Psychology*, Holt, Rinehart & Winston, New York, 1972.

Latané, B., and J. M. Darley: *The Unresponsive Bystander: Why Doesn't He Help?*, Appleton-Century-Crofts, New York, 1970.

Leary, D. E.: One hundred years of experimental psychology: An American perspective, *Psychological Research*, 1980, *42*, 175–189.

Lessac, M. S., and R. L. Solomon: Effects of early isolation on the later adaptive behavior of beagles, *Developmental Psychology*, 1969, *1*, 14–25.

Linsky, A. S.: Stimulating responses to mailed questionnaires: A review, *Public Opinion Quarterly*, 1975, *39*, 83–101.

London, P.: The rescuers: Motivational hypotheses about Christians who saved Jews from the Nazis, in J. Macaulay and L. Berkowitz (eds.), *Altruism and Helping Behavior: Social Psychological Studies of Some Antecedents and Consequences*, Academic Press, New York, 1970.

McGuire, W. J.: Suspiciousness of experimenter's intent, in R. Rosenthal and R. L. Rosnow (eds.), *Artifact in Behavioral Research*, Academic Press, New York, 1969, pp. 13–57.

————: A contextualist theory of knowledge: Its implications for innovation and reform in psychological research, in L. Berkowitz (ed.), *Advances in Experimental Social Psychology*, vol. 16, Academic Press, New York, 1983, in press.

Medawar, P. B.: Induction and Intuition in Scientific Thought, American Philosophical Society, Philadelphia, 1969.

Merton, R. K.: *Social Theory and Social Structure*, enlarged ed., Free Press, New York, 1968.

Murray, H. A.: *Explorations in Personality*, Oxford University Press, New York, 1938.

———: *Thematic Apperception Test*, Harvard University Press, Cambridge, 1943.

Oppenheim, A. N.: *Questionnaire Design and Attitude Measurement*, Basic Books, New York, 1966.

Orne, M. T.: On the social psychology of the psychological experiment: With particular reference to demand characteristics and their implications, *American Psychologist*, 1962, *17*, 776–783.

———: Demand characteristics and the concept of quasi-controls, in R. Rosenthal and R. L. Rosnow (eds.), *Artifact in Behavioral Research*, Academic Press, New York, 1969, pp. 143–147.

———, P. W. Sheehan, and F. J. Evans: Occurrence of posthypnotic behavior outside the experimental setting, *Journal of Personality and Social Psychology*, 1968, *9*, 189–196.

OSS Assessment Staff: *Assessment of Men: Selection of Personnel for the Office of Strategic Services*, Rinehart, New York, 1948.

Palardy, J. M.: What teachers believe—What children achieve, *Elementary School Journal*, 1969, *69*, 370–374.

Pearson, K.: On the mathematical theory of errors of judgment with special reference to the personal equation, *Philosophical Transactions of the Royal Society of London*, 1902, *198*, 235–299.

Pepper, S. C.: *World Hypotheses: A Study in Evidence*, University of California Press, Berkeley, 1942.

Platt, J. R.: Strong inference, *Science*, 1964, *146*, 347–353.

Polanyi, M.: *The Tacit Dimension*, Doubleday Anchor, New York, 1966.

Popper, K. R.: *Logik der Forschung*, Springer Verlag, Vienna, 1934.

———: *The Logic of Scientific Discovery*, Basic Books, New York, 1961.

———: *Conjectures and Refutations*, Routledge & Kegan Paul, London, 1963.

RAND Corporation: *A Million Random Digits with 100,000 Normal Deviates*, Free Press, New York, 1955.

Resnick, J. H., and T. Schwartz: Ethical standards as an independent variable in psychological research, *American Psychologist*, 1973, *28*, 134–139.

Rosenberg, M. J.: The conditions and consequences of evaluation apprehension, in R. Rosenthal and R. L. Rosnow (eds.), *Artifact in Behavioral Research*, Academic Press, New York, 1969, pp. 279–349.

Rosenthal, R.: *Experimenter Effects in Behavioral Research*, Appleton-Century-Crofts, New York, 1966 (enlarged edition, Irvington, 1976).

——: Covert communication in the psychological experiment, *Psychological Bulletin,* 1967, *67,* 356–367.

——: Estimating effective reliability in studies that employ judges' ratings, *Journal of Clinical Psychology,* 1973, *29,* 342–345.

——: Biasing effects of experimenters, *Et Cetera: A Review of General Semantics,* 1977, *34,* 253–264.

——: Conducting judgment studies, in K. R. Scherer and P. Ekman (eds.), *Handbook of Methods in Nonverbal Behavior Research,* Cambridge University Press, New York, 1982. (a)

——: Valid interpretation of quantitative research results, in D. Brinberg and L. Kidder (eds.), *New Directions for Methodology of Social and Behavioral Science: Forms of Validity in Research,* no. 12, Jossey-Bass, San Francisco, 1982. (b)

——, and K. L. Fode: The effect of experimenter bias on the performance of the albino rat, *Behavioral Science,* 1963, *8,* 183–189.

——, and L. Jacobson: *Pygmalion in the Classroom,* Holt, Rinehart & Winston, New York, 1968.

——, and R. Lawson: A longitudinal study of the effects of experimenter bias on the operant learning of laboratory rats, *Journal of Psychiatric Research,* 1964, *2,* 61–72.

——, and R. L. Rosnow: *The Volunteer Subject,* Wiley-Interscience, New York, 1975.

——, and ——: *Essentials of Behavioral Research: Methods and Data Analysis,* McGraw-Hill, New York, 1984.

——, and D. B. Rubin: Interpersonal expectancy effects: The first 345 studies, *The Behavioral and Brain Sciences,* 1978, *3,* 377–386.

——, and ——: A note on percent variance explained as a measure of the importance of effects, *Journal of Applied Social Psychology,* 1979, *9,* 395–396.

——, and ——: A simple, general-purpose display of magnitude of experimental effect, *Journal of Educational Psychology,* 1982, *74,* 166–169.

Rosenzweig, S.: The experimental situation as a psychological problem, *Psychological Review,* 1933, *40,* 337–354.

Rosnow, R. L.: The prophetic vision of Giambattista Vico: Implications for the state of social psychological theory, *Journal of Personality and Social Psychology,* 1978, *36,* 1322–1331.

——: Psychology of rumor reconsidered, *Psychological Bulletin,* 1980, *87,* 578–591.

——: *Paradigms in Transition: The Methodology of Social Inquiry,* Oxford University Press, New York, 1981.

——: Von Osten's horse, Hamlet's question, and the mechanistic view of causality: Implications for a post-crisis social psychology, *Journal of Mind and Behavior,* 1983, *4,* 319–338.

——, and L. S. Aiken: Mediation of artifacts in behavioral research, *Journal of Experimental Social Psychology,* 1973, *9,* 181–201.

————, and R. L. Arms: Adding versus averaging as a stimulus-combination rule in forming impressions of groups, *Journal of Personality and Social Psychology,* 1968, *10,* 363–369.

————, B. E. Goodstadt, J. M. Suls, and A. G. Gitter: More on the social psychology of the experiment: When compliance turns to self-defense, *Journal of Personality and Social Psychology,* 1973, *27,* 337–343.

————, and A. J. Kimmel: Lives of a rumor, *Psychology Today,* 1979, *13,* No. 1, 88–92.

————, H. Wainer, and R. L. Arms: Personality and group impression formation as a function of the amount of overlap in evaluative meaning of the stimulus elements, *Sociometry,* 1970, *33,* 472–484.

Ruch, F. L.: A technique for detecting attempts to fake performance on a self-inventory type of personality test, in Q. McNemar and M. A. Merrill (eds.), *Studies in Personality,* McGraw-Hill, 1942.

Sarbin, T. R.: The logic of prediction in psychology, *Psychological Review,* 1944, *51,* 210–228.

Schuler, H.: *Ethical Problems in Psychological Research*, trans. by M. S. Woodruff and R. A. Wicklund, Academic Press, New York, 1982.

Schultz, D. P.: The human subject in psychological research, *Psychological Bulletin,* 1969, *72,* 214–228.

Sidman, M: *Tactics of Scientific Research: Evaluating Experimental Data in Psychology,* Basic Books, New York, 1960.

Skinner, B. F.: *Science and Human Behavior,* Macmillan, New York, 1953.

Solomon, R. L.: An extension of control group design, *Psychological Bulletin,* 1949, *46,* 137–150.

————, and M. S. Lessac: A control group design for experimental studies of developmental processes, *Psychological Bulletin,* 1968, *70,* 145–150.

Stanley, J. C.: Test reliability, in L. Deighton (ed.), *Encyclopedia of Education,* vol. 9, Free Press and Macmillan, New York, 1971.

Strong, D. R., Jr.: Null hypotheses in ecology, *Synthese,* 1981, *43,* 271–285.

Webb, E. J., D. T. Campbell, R. D. Schwartz, L. Sechrest, and J. B. Grove: *Nonreactive Measures in the Social Sciences,* 2d ed., Houghton Mifflin, Boston, 1981.

Weinstein, D.: Fraud in science, *Social Science Quarterly,* 1979, *59,* 639–652.

Weiss, C. H.: Interaction in the research interview: The effects of rapport on response, *Proceedings of the American Statistical Association: Social Statistics Section,* 1970, 17–20.

Weisskopf, V. F.: The significance of science, *Science,* 1972, *176,* 138–146.

INDEX

185